Russia's Tibet File

The unknown pages in the history of Tibet's independence

by
Nikolai S. Kuleshov

Edited by
Alexander Berzin and John Bray

LIBRARY OF TIBETAN WORKS AND ARCHIVES

First edition 1996

ISBN: 81-86470-05-0

Published by the Library of Tibetan Works and Archives, Dharamsala 176215, India, and printed at Indraprastha Press (CBT), Nehru House, New Delhi-110002.

CONTENTS

Dedication

To my grandson Sviatoslav

PUBLISHER'S NOTE

The Library of Tibetan Works and Archives is pleased to publish *Russia's Tibet File: the unknown pages in the history of Tibet's independence* by Russian historian and author Dr. Kuleshov, who offers a scholarly and insightful glimpse behind the scenes of the political life of Central Asia in the early 20th century. Dr. Kuleshov presents us with new evidence on the involvement of the Russian, British Indian and Chinese governments in the affairs of Tibet.

The relationships between the pivotal figures of the period and place—His Holiness the 13th Dalai Lama, Agvan Dorjiev, Lord Nathaniel Curzon and Sir Francis Younghusband—are explored and given new significance. Basing his work on an analysis of Russian, Indian and British archival material in addition to Chinese reference sources, Dr. Kuleshov has produced a thought-provoking and challenging new interpretation of the events often described previously in works on Tibetan political history.

We trust that readers will find some new materials of interest in this book and realise its full worth as an independent historical study of the overlapping worlds of Tibet, Russia, British India and China.

Gyatsho Tshering
Director, LTWA

August 1996

Photograph from the Jehu collection

His Holiness the 13th Dalai Lama of Tibet

AUTHOR'S PREFACE

Around 100 years ago, international relations in central Asia became the object of close attention by the world press. Public and scientific literature on this issue began to appear during this period; in the present time, that literature and the historical facts it contains are being re-examined.

New conceptions of this subject have been forwarded by this author in papers presented in England, India and Japan, at international conferences of orientalists, and in public discussion at the Royal Academy of the Arts (London, 1992); they were also the basis of discussions between His Holiness the XIV Dalai Lama and myself when His Holiness visited Moscow in 1991. Further to His Holiness' approval, Tibetans have sponsored the translation of this manuscript into English for publication.

Russia's Tibet File: the unknown pages in the history of Tibet's independence is a simplified and condensed version of my detailed monograph *Rossia i Tibet* (*Russia and Tibet*), published in Russian in 1992.

I hope that this condensed work in the English language will be of value to many readers, and that the combination of documentation from the Russian Foreign Policy Archives and my own logical interpretation of events will provide a persuasive thesis.

I am grateful to my colleagues who have corrected the English text, and primarily to Dr. Alexander Berzin and Mr. John Bray who not only edited the manuscript but also overcame some of its shortcomings in the final preparation stages of publication.

DR. N.S. KULESHOV
Moscow, March 1996

Photograph courtesy of John Snelling's estate

Khambo Agvan Dorjiev

Foreword

With the collapse of the totalizing Leninist regime in Russia, the secretly-guarded national archives of the Soviet and Tsarist periods were declared open to the public. This marked not only a milestone in the quest for human freedom; it also proved to be a great boon for scholars, who had been denied access to such official documents for the past 75 years.

Dr. Nikolai Kuleshov celebrates his new-found academic freedom and full access to the Russian Foreign Policy Archives by debunking the 'Great Game' myths. Although one might not entirely agree with the retrospective determinism by which the author goes on to prove his 'thesis', especially in the Introduction, there is no question that the materials he has unearthed from the Russian Foreign Policy Archives constitute a timely and significant contribution to our understanding of the Russian dimension of the 'Great Game' in Inner Asia at the turn of the century. For too long British views and their variations on the subject have dominated the field, mainly because serious scholars (from Alastair Lamb to Parshotam Mehra) did not have access to the Russian records, and worked primarily on the British archival sources.

Now, with the publication of this well-researched monograph, we have no excuse in not understanding the Russian side of the 'Great Game' that allegedly provoked Lord Curzon's forward policy. Dr. Kuleshov's findings throw new light on Imperial Russia's disguised diplomatic activities in and around Tibet, as well as on Agvan Dorjiev's complex motives and intriguing roles. The book also sheds considerable light on the XIII Dalai Lama's lonely struggle for Tibet's freedom. It is interesting to note that his declaration of Tibet's independence in 1912 and the subsequent Tibet-Mongolian Treaty (1913) in which Dorjiev played a crucial role, are well reflected in the Russian archival materials used by our author.

These findings, however, are supposedly side benefits to the academic community, according to the author's intentions. Dr. Kuleshov has a declared 'thesis' to 'prove': that Tsarist Russia never entertained expansionist designs on Tibet; that Agvan Dorjiev was more an agent of the XIII Dalai Lama to the Tsar than a Russian spy in Tibet; and that Lord Curzon's fear of a Russian threat to the Indian empire via Tibet was a case of monumental misperceptions.

Seen from such a perspective, Imperial Russia's keen interest in and disguised involvement with Tibet at the turn of the century were supposedly for the sake of Buryat Buddhists, who followed Tibetan Buddhism and were loyal to the Dalai Lama. This might have been a reinforcing factor but probably not a critical variable, as far as the Tsarist *state* was concerned, it seems.

Indeed, the bulk of evidence presented in this monograph as a whole suggests that Imperial Russia's interest in Tibet went beyond Buryats. It is true that, as a diplomatic practice, Russian state officials always maintained that Russia did not have any direct frontier or military interests in Tibet which seems to be true. But that does not mean Imperial Russia had no strategic interest in Tibet. Russian officials invariably couched their strategic interest in terms of what they called 'moral interests', by which they meant their concern for their Buryat subjects' religious sentiments.

It appears that the imperial powers involved in the 'Great Game' justified their involvement in the strategic rivalry over power-vacuum areas such as Tibet by their 'legitimate interest' claims in the area concerned. Thus, British India did so by its geographical proximity to Tibet; and Tsarist Russia through its Buryat connection. Russia's strategic interest in Tibet becomes clear when we look at an old map of Asia: Tibet was the meeting-point of three rival empires; and because it was a near power-vacuum region, Tibet's geostrategic location easily induced strategic rivalry among the neighboring powers for competitive strategic advantages.

On the surface and in comparison with the strategic interests of China and India in Tibet, those of Russia appear a little remote. However, we must keep in mind the following factors in order to appreciate Imperial Russia's security concerns in Inner Asia: after the conquest of Islamic Central Asia in the 19th century, the Russian empire touched borders close to Tibet. More specifically, Russia's strategic interest in Tibet is, indirectly but effectively, connected with Russian concerns for the stability of their Buryat (lamaist) citizens and with their continued strategic interest in Mongolia. And the Dalai Lama was (and continues to be) a crucial key to Buddhist Central Asia. This is not a new argument; long ago Agvan Dorjiev eloquently presented Tibet's case before the Tsar, arguing along similar lines, as this monograph shows. In short, Tibet at the turn of the century represented (and still does?) a classic security dilemma: the domination of Inner Asia by one neighboring power, creating insecurity for two other neighboring powers.

How else can we understand such weighty state behavior and action that Imperial Russia revealed in relation to Tibet? Agvan Dorjiev enjoyed full access to the Russian Foreign Ministry. Russian Ambassador Benckendorff in London negotiated with his British counterpart for three months in preparation for the 1907 Anglo-Russian Convention on Tibet (that partly resolved the security dilemma through neutralization for 43 years). Russia opened a consulate in Calcutta, the main function of which seemed to have been to watch closely British India's moves towards Tibet. And at the time of the tripartite Simla Agreement (1913-14), Russian Council General Nabokov showed his presence in Simla. All these rich details are presented by Dr. Kuleshov in his book, citing from Russian Foreign Policy Archival records in Moscow.

This is not only a rich Russian contribution, in the post-Soviet era, to the complex history and intriguing politics of early 20th century Tibet; it is also love's labor. The author's admiration for mtsan-nyid mkhanpo Agvan Dorjiev's untiring diplomatic efforts to save the epicentre of his (Dorjiev's) faith from external encroachments is reflected in Nikolai Kuleshov's determination to rehabilitate the Buryat lama as a major actor in Inner Asian history, and not a Russian spy. The author's sympathetic concern for Russia's Buryat Buddhist minority and respect for the present Dalai Lama (whom he met in 1991) reveal his Mahayana motivations to undertake the translation of his *Rossia i Tibet* into English.

Dr. Nikolai Kuleshov believes his rigorous re-examination of the past has certain relevance to the present status of Tibet. He writes that the present Tibetan fate "offends the highest human values--personal liberty and the right of nations to self-determination." He argues that like in the former Soviet Union, "the problem of nationalities was solved in China not on the basis of free expression of the people's will, but by means of force." He pleads for self-determination in the case of Tibet. He also sees another "immediate bond between the past and the present—between the Simla Conference and the McMahon Line on one hand, and the present Sino-Indian border/territorial dispute on the other." Dr. Nikolai Kuleshov appeals to the Government of India to recognize the legality of Tibet's independence in order to defend the legality of the McMahon Line.

DR. DAWA NORBU

Lord George Nathaniel Curzon

Introduction

The first 15 years of the 20th century were a particularly important—perhaps the most important—period in the history of Tibet and the neighboring states. However, international scholarship, in Russia and China as well as in the West, has tended to suffer from two main failings when discussing this period. Firstly, most authors have underestimated Tibet's capacity to decide its own fate, and secondly they have depicted Russia as an aggressor against Tibet. The present study, which is based on an analysis of Russian, Indian and British archives as well as Chinese sources, challenges this version of history.

A rigorous examination of this period is particularly important because of the present condition of Tibet which has been incorporated into the Chinese state, while the Dalai Lama has led a substantial number of his fellow Tibetans into exile. Their fate offends the highest human values—personal liberty and the right of nations to self-determination.

The forces which led to Tibet's present situation were set in motion as a result of the Chinese/Tibetan armed conflict at the beginning of the 20th century. This conflict was itself a consequence of a series of events initiated by two key actors: Agvan Dorjiev, a Buryat of Russian nationality who served as one of the 13th Dalai Lama's advisers in the late 19th and early 20th centuries; and Lord Curzon, the British viceroy of India. At the time observers naturally interpreted the collision of 'Dorjiev versus Curzon' in the light of the preconceptions and prejudices of contemporary politics. Those politics now belong to the past, but they still influence analysis by present-day scholars. It is time for an impartial re-assessment.

This study follows the principle that "the aim of scholarship is truth: the aim of politics is advantage". At the beginning of the 20th century it was natural for political analysis of Tibet to try to prove the correctness of a particular state's foreign policy. The result has been the creation of a number of stereotypes which do not correspond to historical truth. Partly as a result, Lord Curzon has been treated in detail in a number of publications while Agvan Dorjiev has been virtually consigned to oblivion.[1] He is rarely mentioned today and, when he is discussed, his image is often distorted.

TIBET AS A PAWN OF ANGLO-RUSSIAN RIVALRY?

Before discussing the role of individuals, it is important to review some broader themes in the history of Tibet. The critical point is that most historical analysis has tended to assign to Tibet a purely subordinate role, as though it were scarcely capable of influencing its own fate independently. For example, T. Grunfeld's *The Making of Modern Tibet* (London, 1987) views Tibet as an object of manipulation by foreign states: one chapter in the book is entitled "Tibet as a pawn". The source of such misconceptions can be found in the early 20th century when Tibet first became prominent on the wider international scene, and the Great Powers were obliged to formulate their policies towards it.

In 1901 Lord George Hamilton, the British secretary of state for India, wrote to Lord Curzon that Tibet was only an insignificant pawn on the political chessboard but that knights, bishops and castles might all be involved in trying to take it.[2] This metaphor has become a standard expression in historical analysis of Tibet. For example, Grunfeld asserts that at the beginning of the 20th century Tibet was a pawn in the Anglo-Russian struggle for world supremacy.[3]

The thesis that British India and Russia competed for control of Tibet is erroneous. It is undeniable that Anglo-Russian rivalry was a *leitmotif* of 19th century politics, especially during the Crimean war in the 1850s when the British captured the city of Sebastapol, blockaded the Baltic Sea and bombed the Solovetsky monastery. There was fierce competition between the two powers in Asia as well, although it never took the form of armed conflict. However, Anglo-Russian rivalry is far from being the 'key' to unlock all historical puzzles—least of all the Tibetan question.

The traditional version of this thesis states that Russia and Britain had been competing for more than a century. They concentrated their efforts on the seizure of new lands in Asia and established their control through colonization or other forms of influence. By the beginning of the 20th century the interests of the two powers had begun to clash in Tibet. According to this version, England was obliged to protect India from the acquisitive gaze of Russian generals who supposedly aimed to capture Tibet before expanding into India. The literature on this subject is enormous. One bibliography, which confines itself to works in Western European languages appearing before the mid-1970s, cites more than 700 books and articles with a direct bearing on the subject.[4]

However, the archives of the Russian foreign ministry show that Russia did not aspire to Tibet and did its utmost to avoid becoming caught up in Tibetan affairs even though Lhasa's representatives tried for many years to involve St Petersburg in their country's problems. There is not a single document which provides evidence of Russian interest in Tibet from an economic, military or diplomatic point of view.

It is mistakenly thought that Curzon's Tibet policy was influenced by the memory of Anglo-Russian rivalry in Asia during the 19th century. The memory of past rivalries may have helped persuade Curzon's colleagues and superiors to accept his arguments. Even so, the fact that the British Cabinet mistrusted Curzon's warnings of an impending Russian invasion of Tibet shows that the theme of Anglo-Russian rivalry already belonged more and more to the past. Both Britain and Russia were becoming more inclined towards mutual entente.

Meanwhile, the Tibetans had already begun to demonstrate their independence before the beginning of the 20th century. The British and Chinese governments negotiated the 1890 Anglo-Chinese convention and the 1893 Trade Regulations without involving the Tibetans. Precisely for this reason the Tibetans destroyed the boundary posts which had been established on the border between Sikkim and Tibet in accordance with the 1890 convention.

Similarly, the published statistical data show that neither the 1890 nor the 1908 agreement significantly changed the volume of the cross-border trade between India and Tibet. At the beginning of the 20th century senior Indian government figures attached little value to the Indian/Tibetan trade and from their point of view the agreements were at best a declaration of intent. The 1908 agreement was in effect imposed upon the Tibetans and in the years immediately following it the volume of trade fell by half. It remained at this level until 1913 when it again increased. In part this reflected the fact that Tibet had achieved independence, and it signed the 1914 Trade Regulations on its own account, without the participation of the Chinese.

Agvan Dorjiev—the Russian/Tibetan diplomat

Russian historians writing in the 1920s correctly linked Tibet's struggle for independence with the name of Agvan Dorjiev (1854-1938). Khambo Agvan Dorjiev, a Russian Buryat, was both a Buddhist scholar and a statesman. He began his study of Buddhist philosophy when he was 14 and his successful studies attracted the attention of high-ranking Buddhists. They recommended that he pursue his studies and with this in mind he set out first to Urga (now known as Ulan Bator) in Mongolia and then to Lhasa—travelling on foot because there was no other means of transport. In 1880, at the age of 26, Dorjiev found himself in Lhasa. He rose in seniority and acquired a favorable reputation among the country's rulers through hard study combined with his natural ability.

Despite Dorjiev's Russian citizenship, his scholarship and natural intelligence resulted in his appointment as the philosophy tutor of the young Thubten Gyatso, the 13th Dalai Lama. Dorjiev became very close to his pupil, who was 22 years younger. During the previous century almost all the Dalai Lamas had died mysteriously, either shortly before or shortly after taking over the reins of government, thus leaving power in the hands of the regents. Dorjiev did his utmost to preserve the life of the 13th Dalai Lama, who was the first for several generations to survive into adulthood. Once the Dalai Lama assumed control of the government, Dorjiev became one of his key political advisers.

The Russian central government permitted Buryatia a high degree of autonomy, particularly in religious affairs. For Dorjiev Russia was a powerful state which could give Tibet reliable protection combined with independence. He undoubtedly implanted these ideas in his pupil, and they must have influenced the latter's yearning for complete independence from China.

Although Dorjiev was a foreigner, he faithfully and devotedly served Tibet as a statesman for many years, and during this period Tibetans demonstrated their determination to defend their country from outside encroachments. Nevertheless, he is usually presented as a spy, an agent or at best as an intermediary between the Dalai Lama and the Tsar. It is suggested that he was a source of insidious Russian intrigue which turned Tibet into a pawn in the game between Russia and Britain. This portrayal was repeated in Sir Charles Bell's writings on Tibet, while in 1924 the German scientist Wilhelm Filchner published a novel, *Sturm über Asien*, which was loosely based on Dorjiev's life and implied that he had joined the Russian secret service in 1885. Similarly, the American diplomat and historian who published his researches under the name J. MacGregor supposes that Dorjiev was recruited by the Russian secret service when he worked in Przhevalsky's fourth expedition in 1884.[5] However, Dorjiev had nothing to do with Przhevalsky, and it appears that the author has confused him with someone else, just as elsewhere in his bok the confused Cossacks and Kazakhs.[6]

The archives of the Russian foreign ministry show a different picture. Dorjiev's missions to Russia were not secret: they were widely publicized in the press of Russia, England and several other western countries. This lack of secrecy means that Dorjiev can scarcely be characterized as a spy. The documents show that he was not an agent of the Tsar in Tibet but rather an agent of the Dalai Lama to the Tsar, "Lhasa's emissary to the Tsar" according to John Snelling. His mission was to protect the interests of his adopted country, and prevent it coming under the control of external powers. The Tibetans were fully aware of his Russian origin.

Tibet on its own initiative chose Russia as a would-be guarantor of its traditional way of life, but Russia failed to respond—indeed it actively sought to avoid becoming embroiled in Tibetan affairs. This failure is explained not by its obligations to Great Britain or China but rather by the absence of significant Russian interests in Tibet. Nevertheless, Dorjiev's initiatives prompted a reaction first by the British government, which in turn encouraged the Ch'ing government in its ultimately unsuccessful attempts to reassert its control over Tibet. However, every cloud has its silver lining. Tibet was able to achieve much more after being left to its own resources. In 1913 it signed a treaty with Mongolia in which both countries acknowledged each other's independence. In 1914 it took part in the trilateral Simla conference as a full member along with Great Britain and China. None of this would have been possible without Dorjiev's earlier path-breaking diplomacy.

Lord Curzon: Dorjiev's opposite

Lord Curzon, the viceroy of British India, was in many respects Dorjiev's opposite—in culture and background as well as political objectives. Whereas little is known of Dorjiev's ancestry, and many details of his personal history remain obscure, the life of George Nathaniel Curzon (1859-1925) has been widely discussed. Lord Ronaldshay's three-volume *Life of Lord Curzon* appeared as early as 1928, and there have been several other biographies since then.

Curzon was born into an English noble family and studied at Eton and Oxford University. He had a formidable reputation and showed promise as a statesman from the beginning of his career. He had a grand manner, and none but his few intimates knew the witty, friendly and even modest personality behind the facade. As a young man he travelled widely in the East, and published several books and articles about his adventures.

In 1899 Curzon was appointed viceroy of India. This was the same year that Dorjiev undertook his first mission to Russia and from then on the two men's objectives began to clash. Dorjiev's aim was to establish Russia's relations with Tibet: Curzon's priority was to prevent Russia threatening the Indian empire via Tibet.[7]

During his administration in India Curzon clashed with Lord Kitchener, the military commander-in-chief, because he wanted the armed forces to be placed under his control. The clash between the civilian and military authorities was one of the themes of the Younghusband expedition to Tibet.

Russian expansionism?

The growth of Russia's Asian empire in the 18th and 19th centuries has led many to assume that the country was inherently expansionist and in particular that it wished to establish access to the 'warm waters' of the Indian Ocean. The belief that Russia was concerned above all else with access to these 'warm waters' is misleading.

For example, in the late 19th century N.N. Miklukho-Maklai requested the Russian government to establish a protectorate over a part of New Guinea with whose inhabitants he had made friends. The Tsar was shocked to hear that these people wore no trousers because of the warm climate, but he refused to establish the protectorate, not for this reason but because he did not wish the other great powers to accuse him of expansionism. Similarly, in 1901 Kuwait requested Russian patronage and proposed to hoist a Russian flag, but was refused permission. At approximately the same time the Russian poet and traveller N.S. Gumilyov wrote from Djibouti about a Russian who had acquired a small African kingdom and asked his government to admit it to citizenship, but he too was turned down. Dorjiev's diplomacy, which aimed to involve Russia in Tibetan affairs, offered an opportunity to gain access to India and—potentially—to the warm waters to the south. However, Russia did not take this opportunity either.

It is also true that the British government had no expansionist ambitions in Tibet, but an important qualification must be made here. The government of British India frequently disagreed with the home government, especially during the period when Lord Curzon served as viceroy. Curzon advocated a 'forward policy' in

Tibet, although the London government was more cautious, not least because it was concerned at the possible reaction of the Chinese empire.

Curzon tried to pursue his own foreign policy because he was convinced of the superiority of his course of action: he was based in India and was familiar with local conditions whereas London was not, and Tibet was a tempting prize. In order to justify his plans, Curzon revived the idea of Anglo-Russian rivalry over Tibet with such success that his paradigm has dominated most Russian and western historical analysis ever since. However, as Chinese writers have observed, it was not so much Russian expansion that prompted the British expedition into Tibet, but rather the reverse. It was the expedition which forced the Tibetans to seek support from St Petersburg. "Some Tibetan leaders who hated British aggression were inclined to ask Russia for support against England," wrote Liu Danian and his colleagues.[8]

RUSSIAN ARMS IN TIBET?

Several historians refer to Russia's alleged supply of weapons to Tibet. One of Dorjiev's documents—and only one—does refer to Russian arms. Written at the time of the Xinhai Revolution in China, it suggests that Russia should take a number of measures to prevent revolutionary chaos spreading to Tibet. However, the reference to Russian weapons is lost in a discussion of much wider issues. Dorjiev was a diplomat rather than a general, and he was primarily concerned with Russia's political and moral authority rather than its weaponry.

Rumors that Russia was sending rifles to Tibet were started by British colonial officials such as Francis Younghusband and Charles Bell. The Japanese monk Ekai Kawaguchi, who visited Lhasa in disguise, claims to have witnessed the delivery of Russian weapons. In February/March, 1902 he reports that he encountered a caravan of approximately 200 camels which had arrived from the north-east. They delivered boxes covered with skins, and camel-drivers refused to answer questions about their contents. A few days later, a high-ranking Tibetan official told Kawaguchi that Russia had sent rifles and cartridges as a 'gift'. Before the most recent caravan of 200 camels there had been an earlier one of 300 camels. On one of the rifles, Kawaguchi saw the mark 'Made in the USA'.[9] It is unclear how rifles made in the USA could have found their way to Tibet, but worth noting that they were American rather than Russian.

L.A. Waddell, an English author who accompanied the Younghusband expedition to Lhasa, also referred to the rumors of supplies of Russian rifles,[10] but he too cites Kawaguchi as a source, and his reference therefore does not amount to independent corroboration. No more reliable evidence has emerged since then.

In the mid-1920s, Nabokov, an exiled Tsarist diplomat who had been present at the negotiations between Dorjiev and the foreign affairs minister, referred to British concern at Russia's alleged subversion in Tibet as a "comedy of mistakes based on fantasies but not on facts".

Russian consulate in Tachienlu?

Rumors that the Russian government planned to establish a consulate in the eastern Tibetan/Chinese border town of Tachienlu (known to the Tibetans as Dartsendo, and later as Kanding) also have been cited as evidence of Russian ambitions in Tibet. It seems that the Russian foreign ministry did discuss the possibility of establishing a consulate there, and even nominated a certain Rabdanov to occupy it. However, the official directories of the foreign ministry make no reference to the consulate, and there is no evidence that the Russian government took any concrete steps to open it. If it had done, the English would certainly have noticed.

Personal rivalries

The documents which Dorjiev and his contemporaries left in the Russian foreign affairs ministry are not the absolute truth. This is partly because the true situation was often obscure at the time, but also because the documents reflect the personal interests of the authors. As Alistair Lamb comments with regard to Chinese Turkestan (Xinjiang):

> By the beginning of the twentieth century both in London and St Petersburg it had been realized that Anglo-Russian conflict in Kashgaria was often more a personal struggle between Macartney and the Russian Consul-General Petrovsky and his successor Kolokolov, than a fundamental contest of British and Russian interests.[11]

Military expeditions from both sides were exploring the blank spaces on the map at approximately the same time. After meeting the Russian traveller B.L. Grombchevsky in the Pamirs in the 1890s, the British explorer Francis Younghusband wrote that the Russians and the British were rivals, and did not conceal it, but were nonetheless in sympathy with each other. This gentlemanly approach is another reason why the two countries' limited rivalry in Asia did not lead to war.

Religious links between Russia and Tibet

Most of the Buryats, Kalmyks and Mongolians who lived in Russia were Buddhists, and the Dalai Lama was their supreme religious leader. Scholars from these communities travelled to Lhasa to continue their education in the monasteries there. This kind of pilgrimage assisted Russian prestige in Tibet although, as has been seen, it helped foster rumors of Russian subversion there.

A pilgrim Tsar?

Recently, information has become available linking Tsar Alexander I with Tibet. Alexander was one of the outstanding international personalities of the early 19th century, rivalling even Napoleon Bonaparte in his diplomatic skills. He was responsible for the establishment of the 'Holy Alliance' of European monarchs after Napoleon's defeat. Russian legend suggests that Alexander did not die in 1825, as official history records, but took monastic vows and under a new name dedicated himself to God. According to new information, which has not yet been submitted to rigorous scientific examination, he then left for Tibet where he lived for a number of years, becoming immersed in Tibetan culture. After several years, he returned home and settled in Tomsk, remaining incognito. He prayed for forgiveness of his sins, including many carnal ones, and practised Tibetan medicine which he had learned during his travels.

Alexander's religious devotion in the last years of his reign lends plausibility to this story, but it remains unproven and it would be best to treat it as a myth—albeit a particularly captivating one. If it is ever confirmed, then Tibet's links with Russia will be seen to date from earlier in the 19th century, and Dorjiev's activities will be seen more as a natural progression than an aberration.

China's traditional relationship with Tibet

The Great Wall of China was constructed to protect the country from the nomads of the vast Asian steppe. Under Genghis Khan the Mongols united and conquered China, and the Mongolian hordes subsequently reached as far as Europe. The decline of Tartar/Mongolian power did not make China's northern neighbors less warlike, and the empire profited from the authority of the Dalai Lama to help protect it. From the beginning, the Ch'ing dynasty was interested in Tibet not as an object of conquest but rather because of its status as the home of the most senior figures in the Buddhist hierarchy.

The Tibetans requested the Ch'ings to act as patrons of Buddhism because this would help propagate the religion and assist the Dalai Lama in his relations with the Mongolians. Mongolian chronicles describe the Chinese ceremonies on the occasion of the Fifth Dalai Lama's visit to Peking. The emperor met him at a distance of a day's journey from the capital and he entered the city not through the gates but over the city walls. The tops of the walls and the gates were used as streets and it was thought inconceivable that anyone could walk over the head of His Holiness. According to Tibetan chroniclers, the emperor presented the Dalai Lama with a gold dish with the Dalai Lama's title inscribed on it: 'Lord of the Ocean, Ruler of the Thunder'. In response the Dalai Lama also presented a dish with a no less magnificent title: 'Great Sovereign, Lord of Heaven. Bodhisattva'.[12]

Sino-Tibetan relations were based on the mutually beneficial personal relationship between the Dalai Lama and the Chinese emperor. In Lhasa the amban (the emperor's representative) maintained a modest staff and a small armed escort. The Chinese soldiers often married Tibetan women, and their children inherited their father's positions in the escorts. Later on it was difficult to judge whether individual soldiers were Chinese or Tibetans. Moreover, the ambans often were not Chinese but Manchus. Lhasa fenced itself off from political relations with the outside world, claiming that the emperor did not permit this.

THE EMERGING THREAT FROM THE SOUTH

For a time these conventions helped the Tibetan hierarchy to maintain the status quo undisturbed, but by the 19th century the country appeared increasingly vulnerable to external pressure. The Ch'ing court did little to interfere in affairs in the Himalayan region and often was unaware of events there. Meanwhile, the British administration in India was gradually encroaching on territories which came within Tibet's religious, if not political, sphere of influence, and the Chinese did nothing to prevent this. The British fought a war against Bhutan in 1865 and in 1890 Sikkim was officially recognized as a British protectorate under the terms of the 1890 Anglo-Chinese convention.

The 1890 convention called for the demarcation of Sikkim's northern border, but the Tibetans destroyed the boundary markers set up by the British. Historically, the Tibetans had helped establish the authority of the Chögyal (*Chos rgyal*—Dharma-king) of Sikkim. The Sikkimese ruling family continued to intermarry with the Tibetan aristocracy, and Lhasa considered that Sikkim remained a Tibetan dependency. British encroachment on Sikkim was therefore seen as evidence of an emerging threat to Tibet itself. The Tibetans were determined to resist.

Dorjiev played a crucial role in these events because of his close relationship with the 13th Dalai Lama and the fact that he was able to offer a broader international perspective on the outside world. This book is based on hitherto unpublished Russian documents and offers a new perspective on the 13th Dalai Lama's approaches to Russia at the beginning of this century. The author believes that they will be of interest not only to specialists but also to a much wider readership.

Chapter One

Dorjiev's first missions to Russia in 1898-99 and 1901

Although he entered the Dalai Lama's service, Dorjiev always remained a Russian citizen and retained a high respect for his motherland. All his surviving papers testify to his deep personal attachment to his country of origin, and this theme can be seen in his diplomatic activities on Tibet's behalf. Dorjiev's high rank in the Tibetan government was a highly unusual phenomenon, and this raises the question as to how such a thing could have happened. What kind of a person was he, and what role did he play in the Dalai Lama's government?

A Chinese analogy provides part of the answer. In the 19th and early 20th centuries the Chinese empire employed many foreigners. For example, R. Hart, an Englishman, was the head of the Chinese maritime customs service for many decades. Hart and his European colleagues provided the Chinese government with a steady source of income by taxing foreign trade, although they themselves took the lion's share of the profits.[1] The principle of judicious restraint explains why they took only a share and not the whole of the profits. If they had usurped the country outright, the consequences might have contradicted their original objectives because they were not prepared to govern a country as vast as China. The solution was collaboration with the Ch'ing rulers rather than outright annexation. This collaboration was easy to establish because the Chinese authorities were at that time unable to govern without outside assistance and therefore introduced Britons into the power structure in their own self-interest.

The influence of Hart and his staff increased to such an extent that he joined the Empress Dowager and Li Hung-chang (a Chinese dignitary) to form "a powerful trinity" at the head of the Chinese government. Ironically, their presence at the top of the Chinese government influenced British policy on Tibet. British officials acting on China's behalf took part in negotiations on Tibetan questions, and Hart's influence in London was to help frustrate Curzon's Tibet policy.

For all the apparent similarity in their roles, there was a fundamental difference between Hart and Dorjiev. In the long run Hart served the interests of Great Britain. By contrast Dorjiev devoted himself solely to Tibet. London needed its 'man in Peking', and if Hart had not existed some one else would have filled the same role. If Dorjiev had not existed, no one could have replaced him, and Russia's relations with Tibet would have been quite different. His role was all the more important because it took place at a turning point in Tibetan history.

The Tibetans realized that China could not on its own deter the increasing threat from British India. The two ambans, China's representatives in Tibet, tended to be motivated by mercenary considerations and showed little interest in Tibetan affairs of state. Curzon thought that Tibet's links with China amounted to little more than 'political affectation', and were not sufficient to protect the country from foreign invasion.

Liu Guan'i and Huang Fensheng, two Chinese historians writing in the 1950s, confirmed the view that Tibetans had little option but to turn to Russia in their struggle against England, and therefore made contact with Russia on their own initiative.[2] They do not support this judgement with specific citations of Chinese documents, but such documents undoubtedly exist in Chinese state archives which are closed to outsiders.[3]

Dorjiev's own testimony confirms statements made by Chinese sources. Dorjiev explained his mission to Russia by pointing out that the earlier relationship between China and Tibet had broken down, and China was no longer fulfilling its traditional role as Tibet's patron protecting it from its enemies. On the contrary China was exploiting Tibet without giving anything in return. Dorjiev wrote:

> The necessity of seeking the patronage of a foreign country was secretly debated at the highest level in Tibet from the moment when Chinese officials bribed by Englishmen deprived Tibet of the land [this is a reference to the declaration that Sikkim was a British protectorate under the terms of the Anglo-Chinese convention of 1890]. I was present at one such meeting and expressed the opinion that Russia should be given preference.[4]

So Dorjiev championed the idea of turning towards Russia. This change in orientation was dictated by the requirements of Tibet rather than Russia, and Dorjiev himself was at that time quite unknown in the Russian foreign ministry. The ministry was at first naturally surprised to receive a communication from Dorjiev, and started collecting information about him. According to the first documents concerning him in the ministry files:

> Agvan Dorjiev, a Buryat by birth from Trans-Baikal, left for Urga [later Ulan Bator] at the age of 18 and there received Buddhist higher philosophical education before moving to Lhasa.[5]

He rose to prominence comparatively quickly. At the age of 35 he passed an exam to receive the degree of *Lharambo*. Seven teachers were required for the young Dalai Lama, and he was chosen as one of them. He considered Russia to be his motherland, and himself a Russian subject, and he told the Dalai Lama about his origins.[6]

Later, in a detailed account of his origins and of his mission, Dorjiev wrote about his pedigree, his career in Tibet and his difficulties in remaining the Dalai Lama's adviser in spite of demands by influential Tibetans to remove the 'foreigner'. However, he did not give up his idea of projecting a favorable view of his motherland and winning Tibetan sympathy for everything Russian. Thus the Tibetans received good information about Russia, while remaining comparatively ignorant about other countries.

In 1888 the French Prince Henri of Orleans visited Tibet with a view to opening diplomatic relations. In a message to the Tibetan government he promised, "We, the French, can save Tibet from the English threat. France and Russia have concluded an alliance, and are now the strongest powers in the world." Dorjiev wrote that the prince's words served to confirm his reports of Russian power, and the Tibetan 'Tsar' and other officials began to request more information about Russia and Europe as a whole. Increasing evidence that the Ch'ing dynasty was close to collapse made such information all the more urgent.

However, the Tibetans wished to act circumspectly. According to Dorjiev, a number of Lhasa officials had been impressed by his stories of Russia's might, but became somewhat distrustful of his information after hearing the prince's captivating stories about France. The Lhasa government decided to send a mission to Russia, but its scope was limited. The officials accompanying Dorjiev merely wished to become acquainted with the way of life in China,

Russia and France at first hand.[7] They decided to travel to St Petersburg via India, China, Mongolia and Buryatia.

Senior Russian figures in commerce, politics and the court did not consider relations with the Far East to be a high priority. When Dorjiev appeared in St Petersburg in 1899, the first reaction of some Russian statesmen was to send a representative to Tibet. This proposal seemed straightforward but, from the Tibetan point of view, it was premature: they had only just begun to consider re-orienting their foreign policy. Dorjiev explained that at least two missions would be required to win Tibet's favor.8

In their preliminary talks with Dorjiev, Count Lamsdorff, Count Witte and General Kuropatkin suggested that Russia should open a consulate in Tibet. However, the Tibetan delegation had neither the authority to accept this proposal nor a clear view that it was desirable. As Dorjiev explained, "Having allowed Russians to enter the country, Tibet would not be able to withstand the influx of other Europeans." His aim was to establish Russia's pre-eminence while at the same time excluding any other foreign presence in Tibet.

Such caution was natural for the Tibetans, given the importance of the issues. However, their Russian sponsors, who had no great interests at stake, saw their response as irresolute and hestitant, and this undoubtedly affected the further development of Dorjiev's initiative. Dorjiev confined himself to sounding out the possibility of realizing Tibetan plans through a link with Russia and sent a letter to the Dalai Lama which "described in detail the greatness of the Russian people and the critical position of China, adding that the connection with Russia promised a great future for Tibet." [9]

Dorjiev then left for Western Europe, but did not stay there for long. He met French connoisseurs of Buddhism, and hundreds of people attended his lectures on the religion and traditions of the Chinese, Mongolians and Buryats. After returning to Russia, Dorjiev asked Russian orientalists to arrange his meeting with the Tsar. Prince Ukhtomskiy, whom Dorjiev had first met in Buryatia, went with him to the Tsar's summer residence at Livadia in Crimea. Dorjiev was granted an audience with the emperor but, being alone and lacking documentary authority, he was treated as a private person. Without making any particular claims, he drew attention to the connections between the Russian orthodox church, which had good relations with Buddhists in Buryatia, Kalmykia, Stavropolie and other places. On Solovetsky Island, guides still show tourists the dog-rose bushes which were cultivated from seeds sent by the Dalai Lama.

Soon the Dalai Lama insisted on Dorjiev returning to Tibet. His journey took him through Peking, Calcutta, Darjeeling and Sikkim. This was the usual route to Tibet, and even Chinese officials followed it because it was quicker and safer than travelling overland from China Dorjiev returned to Lhasa on February 28, 1901. He found that the Dalai Lama had passed his St Petersburg correspondence to his ministers. One group of ministers found it inappropriate to search for an alliance other than from France, which had been the first to propose establishing relations. Dorjiev wrote that, "Others consider that it would be wiser to make friends with the English because such neighbors could make a great deal of trouble if they became enemies. However, the majority held the view that it would be better to address Russia where Buddhism prospered freely." Their former uncertainty with regard to the choice of a protector had disappeared, and there was a strong view that Tibet had at last found a protector more reliable than China.[10]

Thus, Tibet turned to Russia because of the urgent need to obtain the support and patronage of a large, modern state and after reviewing a range of candidates to play this role. The Dalai Lama saw that Tibet had no choice but to seek protection either from the north or the south: he was determined to choose Russia.[11]

In recognition of his services Dorjiev was promoted to the rank of senior *Khamba*, and the Tibetan government decided to send a second delegation to Russia with a view to conducting official negotiations. Dorjiev left Lhasa at the head of this mission on March 29, 1901. Among others, its members included several high-ranking Tibetans: Kainchok,[12] the second secretary of the Dalai Lama and district chief Pintsok. The Tibetans carried a letter to the Tsar and gifts from the Dalai Lama in accordance with the traditions of Asian diplomacy.

From India the Tibetans travelled by sea to Vladivostok and then up the river Amur. They were deeply distressed at the sight of settlements destroyed on the Chinese bank of the river. Dorjiev described Aigun, a large Chinese town where all the citizens had been killed and the town itself burnt down and destroyed. He felt that here human beings had shown themselves more savagely cruel than beasts. This encounter strengthened his determination to achieve peace and stability in Tibet with the help of Russia.

Having arrived in St Petersburg, Dorjiev wrote to the Tsar to request an audience. He wrote that recent changes in China had led some members of Tibet's ruling circle to advise an approach to England, "while others found it more profitable to ask France for protection, and a third group insisted on the support and patronage of Russia under whose mighty dominion Buddhists had prospered. The last opinion had triumphed, and all the Tibetans had decided to ask the Russian Tsar for protection."[13]

The prosperity of Buddhists in Russia could not have been the sole reason for Tibet's choice of Russia, since Buddhists also were free from oppression in British India and French Indo-China. Their preference for Russia was justified by the latter's remoteness. Dorjiev later wrote in his autobiography that the Tibetans had chosen Russia because on the one hand its political might offered protection while, more importantly, it was too far away to present a direct threat on its own account. Dorjiev did not mention this argument in his official dealings with Russia.

However, one should bear in mind that the decision to approach Russia did not come easily to the Tibetans. For centuries their leaders had saved the country from outside political influence (apart from the Ch'ing ambans and the Nepali and central Asian merchants who maintained traditional trade links with Lhasa). Both the Tibetan rulers and the Chinese ambans were hostile to everything foreign. Schekin, a Russian official who met Dorjiev when he arrived in Russia reported to his superiors that "Tibet's reserve and aversion towards foreigners is intensified by the Chinese who paint the disastrous results of the penetration of overseas barbarians in China in dark colors to the local inhabitants."[14]

The letter which Dorjiev brought from the Dalai Lama was written in Tibetan and Mongolian. It was sent to St Petersburg University to be translated, but not to the Russian foreign affairs ministry, and this indicates that the ruling circles in St Petersburg had decided not to pay much attention to it. The Mongolian text was translated but not the Tibetan one because there were no Tibetan linguists in the university. The letter did not contain any direct requests for protection or political patronage but merely stated:

> Your Majesty does not reject those professing numerous religions and in particular you take care of Kalmyks and Buryats.[15]

The Russian government showed extreme restraint from the very beginning of Lhasa's attempts to open relations with St Petersburg.

The Tsar's memorandum proposed to pay little attention to Dorjiev's visit and as far as possible to limit the amount of time he stayed in the country:

> Since it would be inconvenient to give Dorjiev a written answer to the Dalai Lama's petitions, there is apparently no reasons to delay the latter's messenger, who hastens to return to Tibet.

In Russia Dorjiev was received with the honor befitting his high rank as the Dalai Lama's representative. By imperial command he was presented with "free passage by Russian means of transport and all possible conveniences during his journey".[16] However, Dorjiev's mission made little impact in official circles. The double-headed eagle in Russia's state emblem looked in both directions (east and west), but Russian diplomacy was focused primarily on the West. [17]

The Tsar's reply on July 1, 1901 diplomatically informed the Dalai Lama:

> It was a pleasure to learn of your wish to establish permanent relations between Russia and Tibet, and I have given all possible explanations on this subject to your ambassadors.

As can be seen, the Tsar's reply to the Dalai Lama was evasive and undoubtedly disappointed Dorjiev. But the Tsar's reaction was not unexpected given the direction of Russia's foreign policy. In addition to the Dalai Lama's letter, the Tibetan mission also delivered to St Petersburg a letter from the chief manager of the Dalai Lama's palace and the Kalons (Tibetan ministers). This said:

> When the English foreigners began to show hostility towards the Tibetan state as well as the *Bogdykhan* [the Chinese emperor] and with no sympathies and aspirations as regards the hostile Englishmen, we specially sent close servants of the Dalai Lama with a view to uniting Russians and Tibetans in peace and joining them together as though they were in one family.[18]

The Russian foreign ministry handed Dorjiev a reply declining the Tibetans' request to join together in one family. The minister wrote:

> I did not fail to explain in detail, with the assistance of your ambassadors, the means of establishing communications

> with Tibet, and I hope that the measures taken and the results achieved will fully correspond to your wishes. I do not doubt that, according to your wise and careful wishes, no harm will come to Tibet given Russia's invariable benevolence towards it.

Thus, neither the Tibetans' appeal to the Tsar nor to the government fulfilled their hopes. The foreign affairs ministry's reply was as evasive as that of the Tsar. The Russian foreign policy establishment as a whole showed no interest in the Tibetan proposal to establish official bilateral relations even though Russia would not have lost anything by accepting it. The Tibetans stressed that their approach to Russia would not have damaged the latter's relations with China.

The Russian government had no intention of deriving benefit from Dorjiev's mission. The Russian foreign affairs ministry invariably informed British officials about the contents of Russian-Tibetan negotiations, including the details of Dorjiev's conversation with the Tsar. The British Foreign Office in turn informed the British press. However, the press was influenced by the stereotype of Anglo-Russian rivalry which had been formed in previous decades. *The Times* of London wrote that the mission and the exchange of gifts between the Tsar and the Dalai Lama was to Britain's detriment and the formation of a bilateral alliance would certainly be against British interests. Although the question of an alliance between Russia and Tibet was not in fact discussed at the meetings, British newspapermen already regarded it as a reality. This interpretation was a response not to real events but to preconceptions on the nature of Anglo-Russian relations which had formed in earlier years.

However, *Times* correspondents in Russia attached much less significance to Dorjiev's mission. According to its Odessa correspondent, who witnessed the arrival of the mission, the members were welcomed with genuine Russian cordiality and presented with bread and salt on a gilded tray, a traditional Russian ceremony to welcome honored guests. This made a deep impression on the lamas.[19] Dorjiev's mission was described in detail in the Russian press, beginning with the newspapers of Odessa where the mission arrived from Ceylon on board the steamer 'Tambov'. Local newspapers added their own exotic fantasies. For example, the *Odesskiye Novosti* wrote that the town's administration arranged a special celebration in honor of the mission:

> By the time the mission arrived, all the platforms at the station were overcrowded. An orchestra was playing. Tea and refreshments were arranged in the garden, which was full of resort visitors. But the members of the mission do not smoke or drink alcohol. At 11 pm there was a brilliant firework display finishing with the Dalai Lama's initials shining in golden letters against the black sky. Before the mission left for the town, its leader was presented with a splendid bouquet of white roses with a suggestion that this color, a symbol of peace, should be a token of peaceful relations between Russia and Tibet.[20]

Similarly, the *Odessi Listok* newspaper reported colorful details, surely invented, about one of the Tibetan delegates' impressions:

> We know that in Russia besides tea, fruit and soft drinks, there are other national delicacies known as *vodka* and *hors d'oeuvre*. However, we were not invited to taste them first because of the language difficulty and then because someone floated an absurd rumor that Tibetans do not drink anything but water. These must be dirty tricks played by Englishmen.

There were some serious newspaper reports in addition to the more entertaining ones. The St Petersburg *Novoye Vremya*, being a semi-official organ, wrote much about the mission and discussed its implications from various points of view. Some of its articles differed from the official line and represented the opinions of venturesome groups around the government who tried to make capital out of the mission. Russia's foreign policy-makers regarded Dorjiev's mission as a religious delegation, and had no political views on Tibet: they reprimanded the newspaper's publishers for broadcasting those articles. However, the foreign affairs ministry had no authority to apply any sanctions to *Novoye Vremya*, and the incident came to nothing more than a serious reprimand which damaged the newspaper's reputation.

In spite of the quantity of public information about Dorjiev's mission in the Russian and foreign press, historians have tended to describe it as 'secret'. For example, the well-known Tibetologist J. Kolmaš writes: "Dorjiev was entrusted with more than one secret mission from the Dalai Lama to Tsar Nicholas."[21] However, neither the missions themselves nor their contents were secret to anybody.

The Tibetan side wanted to avoid publicity and fuss on the occasion of Dorjiev's missions since they were concerned with important state objectives. However, their Russian partners did not consider it necessary to conceal anything. The Tibetans knew that, because of Lord Curzon's influence, the British press would describe the Tibetan initiative in hostile terms, and they wanted to avoid any resulting complications. One of the documents reports:

> After the audience, Dorjiev was anxious to return to Tibet as fast as possible, because he feared that too long a stay in Russia would lead to undesirable comment in the foreign press.

Indeed, not only British newspapers but also the press of other countries reported on the mission. A series of articles published in the summer of 1901 in the *Japan Times* attached considerable importance to it. A Russian diplomat from Tokyo wrote:

> According to the views represented in these articles, Dorjiev's mission indicates Russia's crafty new plans, and this must prompt Japan to pay special attention to Tibet.

The Buryat Lamas, who belonged to the same stock as Dorjiev himself, put pressure on him to return to Tibet as soon as possible. The lamas occupied an ambiguous position with respect to the Tsarist government. On the one hand the Buddhist hierarchy wanted to testify its loyalty to the tsars. On the other hand, 19th century religious literature published in the Datsangs maintained that everything 'Russian' was unacceptable. Dorjiev was an educated man and therefore was aware of this literature although, as he pointed out in his speech to the Tsar, he knew that the Buryats did not suffer from any form of political oppression. Indeed, the Buryat lamas derived considerable benefit from the Russian government's recognition of their religion. The fact that the lamas were able to balance the Dalai Lama's authority against the Tsar's increased their sense of independence. Dorjiev's aim of linking Lhasa and St Petersburg could have curtailed this independence.

CHAPTER TWO
Curzon's reaction

Lord Curzon, the viceroy of India, responded sharply to news of Dorjiev's visit to Russia even though the St Petersburg government had rejected the proposal to establish bilateral diplomatic relations and had decided that it was "undoubtedly necessary to preserve the status quo in Tibet".[1] As the American orientalist Owen Lattimore later commented, the British wished to maintain the prestige of their empire and therefore wished to make sure that their Indian subjects did not become aware of another empire comparable with their own.[2]

This was very much Curzon's point of view. In order to frustrate Tibetan plans he again began to propagate the long-standing view that the 'Russian menace' threatened Asia. A series of press reports supported his opinion, and an extensive diplomatic correspondence ensued first between Calcutta and London, and then between London and other capitals in Western Europe. A background of Anglo-Russian rivalry over other issues meant that Curzon's arguments were all the more likely to be believed.

In April, 1902 the Reuters news agency reported that de Lessare, the Russian ambassador in Peking, had suggested to Prince Ch'ing, one of the main figures in the politics of the Ch'ing empire, that China should grant Tibet independence. Later rumors emerged concerning a Russian/Chinese treaty on Tibet. It was said that the treaty consisted of 11 articles including the following terms: China would give up its rights in Tibet and in return Russia committed itself to maintaining the unity of the Ch'ing empire.

No documents in the Russian foreign affairs ministry support this rumor, and even contemporaries doubted the existence of the treaty. For example, Sir Ernest Satow, the British minister in Peking, reporting on yet another variant of the alleged Russian/Chinese treaty, wrote that he himself had no reason to believe that such a document existed. In an interview with Satow, Prince Ch'ing had insisted that the treaty was a newspaper hoax.[3]

However, despite Prince Ch'ing's assurances, statements by more junior Ch'ing officials served to reinforce the rumors. For example, The British Political Officer in Sikkim reported that the

Chinese amban in Lhasa had expressed his personal view that the Tibetans would again appeal to Russia, which had already offered assistance, if the Indian government insisted on demarcating the Sikkimese border in accordance with the 1890 convention.

In the view of Lord Curzon's government in Calcutta, Dorjiev was undoubtedly a Russian agent. Francis Younghusband, a prominent British official who later led the British military expedition to Tibet, drew up a memorandum for the foreign secretary of the Indian government discussing Russian attempts to reach Lhasa. The memorandum reported that many Russian military/scientific expeditions had tried to reach the city over the previous 30 years, although none succeeded because they had encountered armed obstacles en route to Lhasa and had been forced to withdraw. Przhevalsky, Pevtsov, Roborovsky and Kozlov all returned to Russia empty-handed even though they had been supplied with official Chinese passports. However, Younghusband concluded that the Russian officers remained full of enthusiasm for studying Tibet.[4]

According to Przhevalsky, the members of his expedition had used "money, whip and bullet" to defend themselves, but had nevertheless been forced to turn back only 200km from Lhasa because Tibetan government officials refused to accept his Chinese certificates. This incident testifies to the ineffectiveness of the Chinese presence in Tibet.

Besides the Russian travellers, Buryat Buddhist pilgrims also visited Tibet, and this gave rise to rumors that they had been engaging in espionage. Younghusband referred to the travels of "Siberian lamas" in his memorandum. According to him, one Badmaev had reached Lhasa in 1899 and had given rich presents to the Dalai Lama. A Kalmyk called Norzunov, who had a Stavropol certificate and an introductory letter from the Russian and French geographical societies, had also visited Lhasa and published photographs of his travels. Tsibikov, a Buryat, visited Lhasa and returned with 319 volumes of Buddhist philosophy, an acquisition which was regarded as one of the greatest achievements of the Russian Geographical Society. Incidentally, Nurzunov later brought a letter from Dorjiev to the Dalai Lama describing his first impressions of his visit to St Petersburg.

The Russians also permitted return visits. The Russian interior minister wrote about one such case to Lamsdorff, the foreign minister:

> Concerning the application by the Tibetan lama Loavsan Jimo for permission to stay in the Trans-Baikal region: he arrived in the empire's territory to teach the Buryat lamas the highest doctrines of Buddhism on behalf of the Dalai Lama. According to a report from the Trans-Baikal governor, the said lama has been living in the region for two years already, has given no cause for complaint, and is permitted to stay indefinitely.[5]

The Russian journeys to Tibet which Younghusband describes were far from extraordinary. Travellers from other countries included: Bonvalot, Dutreuil de Rhins and Grenard from France; Rockhill from the United States; Rijnhardt from the Netherlands; the Schlagintweit brothers from Germany; Kawaguchi from Japan; and Hedin from Sweden. However, none of these were able to reach Lhasa. As Younghusband pointed out, the Chinese passports which they carried made no impression on the Tibetans. It should be pointed out that these journeys also raised the suspicions of the British in India even though the travellers often were furnished with letters of recommendation from the governments and learned societies of their own countries.

In response to Curzon's persistent queries, Lord George Hamilton (the secretary of state for India) reported that the Marquess of Lansdowne (the foreign secretary) had asked the Russian ambassador about his government's intentions towards Tibet. The ambassador had replied that there was no convention between Russia and Tibet or between Russia and China concerning Tibet; that the Russian government had no agents in Tibet; and that it had no intention of sending any. He even expressed surprise that the question should be asked.[6]

However, Curzon continued to press London on the subject of Russian/Tibetan relations. In March 1903, the Russian foreign affairs minister wrote to his ambassador in London wondering whether Lansdowne's queries on Russia's intentions in Tibet were some sort of joke designed to conceal his own intrigues: it was difficult to imagine that the foreign secretary, who was acquainted with conditions in Tibet, could have been seriously worried about the imaginary Tibetan convention with Russia.[7]

Indeed, London did not take the viceroy's concerns particularly seriously, and its indifferent response prompted British officials in India to take a more aggressive stance. For example, Captain O'Connor, a political officer, proposed sending a delegation to the Dalai Lama together with a military escort. Simultaneously, it would notify the Chinese amban of the declaration of war between Britain and China with a view to helping Tibet "throw off the Chinese yoke".[8]

Such suggestions could only have come from British officials in India rather than their colleagues in London because the home government placed a higher value on peaceful relations with China than on anxieties concerning Tibet. The idea of assistance to Tibet was in effect a euphemism standing for Tibet's military usurpation. U.B. Robertson, chief assistant to the Indian army's general headquarters, estimated that this would be a straightforward exercise with little prospect of effective resistance either from "powerless China" or "the greedy lamas".[9] The Indian foreign affairs department reported:

> The so-called Tibetan army consists nominally of 6,000 people. Only half of them serve in the forces and the others are occupied with their own business. They are armed with swords and lances. There are several separate Chinese garrisons, but they have no military significance. Many of them are armed with bows and arrows; the others do not have arms at all.[10]

The viceroy believed that the alpha and omega of Russian policy was "keeping England quiet in Europe by making it anxious in Asia", and he did his utmost to prevent Russia gaining an advantage in Tibet at the expense of the British. The correspondence between the viceroy's staff and London shows that Curzon stressed the necessity of establishing a British mission in Lhasa (thus justifying Dorjiev's observation during his preliminary talks in St Petersburg that the establishment of a Russian mission would lead to demands for similar privileges by other powers). However, London did not support Curzon in this.

Despite London's restraint Curzon persisted in his concerns. He drew an analogy with the negotiations between Dorjiev and Russia, and proposed that the British should enter into their own negotiations with Tibet. This proposal marks the beginning of a process whereby British approaches to Tibet escalated from diplomatic initiatives to a full-scale military expedition.

Curzon's proposals were prefaced by an extensive analysis of the Tibetan question, with the conclusion that there was only one solution. His principal conclusion was that there was little point in negotiations with the Tibetans or the Chinese which focused solely on trade or the Sikkimese/Tibetan border, since the main issue was the status of Tibet. The 'fiction' of Chinese control of Tibet and the Tibetan policy of isolation were admissible only if they did not contain the elements of political and military danger. The possibility that Russia might establish a protectorate over Tibet demanded an entirely different approach. In Curzon's view it was necessary to inform the Chinese that the English intended to open negotiations in Lhasa in the spring of 1903, and a properly briefed Tibetan representative should take part. The time was particularly suitable for such negotiations since the present Dalai Lama was "neither an infant nor a puppet" for the first time for over a century. It should be possible to discuss not only the relatively minor Sikkim border issue but the whole problem of trade and other relations with Tibet and as a result to appoint a permanent consulate or diplomatic mission in Lhasa.

Curzon suggested that the British mission should be accompanied by a military escort in case of Tibetan attack. It should be presented as a trade mission with a view to assuring the Chinese and the Tibetans that the British had no intention of establishing a protectorate over Tibet or capturing it either partially or completely.[11]

The London government sympathized with the plan as Curzon presented it. His intention to draw the Tibetans into negotiations seemed appropriate not only because of Dorjiev's talks in St Petersburg but also because experience had shown that agreements with China over Tibet had no practical outcome. If the Tibetans participated in negotiations, they would feel bound to stand by any subsequent agreements.

The Chinese authorities did not object to direct negotiations with the Tibetans. In January 1903 the Manchu amban in Lhasa wrote to J. Claude White, the British Political Officer for Sikkim, suggesting that he come to Yatung for a few days to settle the frontier question and other issues amicably (Yatung was the only place in Tibet to which British subjects had access under the terms of the Anglo-Chinese convention of 1890 and the Trade Regulations of 1893). However, White did not go to Yatung because he had no instructions from his superiors to this effect.

Having received no reply, the amban sent another letter expressing concern that his former proposal had been unacceptable and showing his "readiness to come to negotiations at the place most convenient for the viceroy". In his next letter the amban wrote to the viceroy that the Chinese representatives had frozen their heels in Yatung for three months expecting the beginning of negotiations. He also offered to come to Sikkim or any other place depending on the viceroy's decision.[12]

The amban's persistent attempts to enter into negotiations with the participation of the Tibetans contrast with later Chinese rhetoric concerning 'imperialist aggression' against Tibet. However, contemporary Chinese historical writing shows that the Ch'ing government wanted to use foreign powers to achieve its own objectives in Tibet. It believed that co-operation with foreign powers was the best way of maintaining its feudal domination over Tibet.[13] Numerous documents by Chinese officials at various levels show that the Chinese side viewed British activities in Tibet rather favorably.

The weakness of the Chinese position was that the Tibetans distrusted them and therefore were unlikely to respond to their influence. The British minister in Peking wrote:

> I am disposed to think that the Chinese government is really desirous of seeing the matter brought to a satisfactory conclusion between India and Tibet, but from Prince Ch'ing's (the Chinese foreign minister) repeated allusion to the obstinate temper of the Tibetans and the difficulty the Imperial Resident (i.e. amban in Lhasa) experiences in dealing with them, they are not sanguine as to the likelihood of Yu Tai's being able to expedite the negotiations[14] "since the Tibetans always considered the amban to be adherent of the English."[15]

The Indian government chose Khamba Dzong, a Tibetan settlement near the Sikkim border, as the site of negotiations. Curzon's plan was to send a mission with a military escort to "make the Dalai Lama recognize the government of British India and stop his flirtation with the Russians." At the same time it would put an end to Chinese claims to command the Tibetan regime.

However, the London government remained opposed to the colonization of Tibet because this would have been inconsistent with the wider objectives of British foreign policy. The British government still considered Tibet to be one of the smallest pawns on the international chess board, but nevertheless avoided reckless actions. Lord Hamilton, the secretary of state for India, knew Curzon well and distrusted his information on the Russian threat.

Eventually, London and Calcutta reached a compromise: they would send a British mission to Khamba Dzong with a view to discussing the Sikkimese/Tibetan border as well as trade issues.

Having received permission to send his mission to Tibet, Curzon felt that he had been given the scope he needed. By adopting a strong position at the negotiations, and frightening the Chinese and the Tibetans, he intended to dictate conditions to them. If the negotiations in Khamba Dzong failed, he expected that the London government would be unable to prevent the mission penetrating deeper into Tibet.

Chapter Three

The Younghusband expedition to Tibet, 1903-1904

The British government in London did not at first allow the mission to penetrate deep into Tibet: it considered that its purpose was the resolution of the Sikkim-Tibet border question and various trade issues rather than the occupation of Tibet. However, Curzon acted independently of London's orders.

In the summer of 1903, Curzon appointed Major Francis Younghusband, an old participant in the central Asian 'Great Game', as head of a frontier commission to negotiate these issues with the representatives of the Dalai Lama and the Chinese amban in Lhasa. In order to increase the mission's authority, Younghusband was promoted to colonel for the duration of the negotiations. Younghusband was a typical British colonial official: he had been born in India and had studied first at Clifton College, a public school in Bristol, and then at the military academy in Sandhurst.[1] He was 19 years old when he began military service in the Royal Dragoons. In addition to his military career he fulfilled various political assignments. The range of his interests was very wide: besides the exploration of the Himalayas, he devoted much attention to mysticism and he later wrote some 20 books, including several dedicated to Tibetan issues.

In theory, Curzon's actions could be explained by a desire to take advantage of Dorjiev's negotiations in St Petersburg to correct the past mistakes of British India in its handling of the northern border. This raises the question: if there had been no Dorjiev, would Curzon have behaved in the same way? The answer must be that he would have done so, possibly even more decisively. And one can be sure that Curzon himself did not believe in the Russian menace to Tibet. London did not believe in it either: the political climate in Europe was beginning to change and within a few years England and Russia were to enter a period of *entente*. Curzon was so preoccupied with Asian affairs that he did not appreciate the nuances of developments in Europe. Although Curzon did not really believe in the Russian menace in Tibet, he wanted to convince

London that such a menace existed so that the government would give him permission to carry out his own policies on Tibet.

Dorjiev's mission helped justify Curzon's plans which went beyond trade and border issues—as later became clear from the conduct of Younghusband's mission. Even at the beginning it was clear that trade prospects were limited given the semi-subsistence nature of the Tibetan economy. Referring to Curzon's arguments, D. Fitzpatrick, a member of the Indian council in London, wrote that the trade was worth nothing and that there was no need to know Lord Curzon's opinion on the issue.[2] Similarly, Clemm, the Russian consul in Bombay, pointed out in his report to St Petersburg:

> The Indian government [i.e. Curzon's administration] hopes soon to gain access for Indian goods to the forbidden country not so much for commercial profits, which will scarcely be significant given the poverty and small population of Tibet, but rather for the expansion of its own influence in the country.[3]

The colonial administration in India actively propagated an anti-Tibetan stance. The *Pioneer*, a prominent Indian newspaper, wrote on 13 October 1903:

> Since the time of the Chinese-Japanese war of 1894, the influence of Peking in Tibet had diminished and Lhasa has demonstrated its independence from its suzerain more than once. The Chinese amban the other day complained to the Empress Dowager that he was quite ignored by the Tibetan officials. He wrote that the "rudeness, ignorance and audacity of the Tibetans were well-known and he was unable to ensure their obedience." It is quite clear that the Tibetans condemned the 1890 convention, which testifies to the fact that Lhasa ignored the Chinese rulers...There is every reason to believe that Lhasa, having thrown off the Chinese yoke, would like Russia to take the place of the 'son of heaven'. Intrigues and pressure (on the part of Russia) to win influence are taking place everywhere. St Petersburg and Lhasa have exchanged friendly messages. The ultimate objective is undoubtedly the Russification of Tibet. The Lhasa lamas, being ignorant of international affairs, do not understand the British government. In several months they will

realize that no one will save them from the consequences of their own obstinacy.

When the negotiations in Khamba Dzong were underway in the summer and autumn of 1903, the English and the Chinese acted with mutual understanding. The English doubted that the Lhasa administration would appoint officials with sufficient authority to negotiate. In order to eliminate these doubts, the Foreign Office instructed the British ambassador in Peking to insist on the Chinese representatives being accompanied by accredited Tibetan representatives. The Ch'ing government instructed the amban accordingly, and assured the English that it had done its utmost to fulfil this condition while at the same time pointing out the barbarian nature of the Tibetans. In an address to the Lhasa Kalons (ministers) the amban admonished the Tibetan 'barbarians', told them that it would be advisable to start negotiations with the English and exhorted them not to resist the latter by force even if they entered Tibet. These exhortations evidently helped, at least temporarily, and the Dalai Lama appointed two Tibetan delegates.

Although Younghusband questioned the seniority of his negotiation partners, he decided—after hesitating for three days—to open the session and to deliver a speech to these 'miserable representatives'. However, before he had done so, the Tibetans put forward their objections. They objected to Khamba Dzong as the site for negotiations: Younghusband's explanation that the place had been chosen by the amban and the viceroy made no impression. Besides, the Tibetans objected to the Englishman's huge military escort: they pointed out that since the negotiations were peaceful the presence of the large number of soldiers was incomprehensible.

The Chinese delegate Ho Kuang-Hsi explained to Younghusband that the Tibetans were ignorant and that it was difficult to deal with them. However, all his efforts were brought to nothing by the Tibetans. The first meeting of the three governments' delegates turned out to be the last one. They stayed in Khamba Dzong for the next three months but, rather than carrying out negotiations, they invariably expressed their wish that the British force withdraw from Tibetan territory back into India. Younghusband asked for permission to use force against the Tibetans, but Curzon refused to give it without authorization from London. Curzon wrote that they were tied hand and foot by the government.[4]

From the very beginning, the British representatives were not serious about the negotiations in Khamba Dzong: they were preparing grounds for the advance to Lhasa. One justification for ending the Khamba Dzong meetings was that the representatives on the Tibetan side were not sufficiently senior. Younghusband arrived at the negotiations with the rank of major. Even before the negotiations started, he expressed doubts about the authority of the Tibetan delegation. Now he pointed out that his negotiation partners were low-ranking and the Chinese should have sent the deputy amban and the Tibetan government a member of the state council.

The Tibetan delegates' objections to the presence of British armed forces on Tibetan territory in Khamba Dzong and their refusal to listen to Younghusband's introductory speech were intended for the Tibetan government in Lhasa. Even their refusal to accept the text of the speech indicated that the Tibetans had no plenipotentiary powers. Younghusband's unwillingness to negotiate with the Tibetans was intensified by the fact that Ho Kuang-Hsi, the Chinese representative, had not the slightest influence upon the Tibetans: his prime concern was to finish this troublesome business as soon as possible and return home. Although Curzon did not authorize Younghusband to resort to force, more and more factors appeared to justify such an approach.

The British cabinet authorized Curzon to proceed into Tibet, but subject to several conditions, especially that the proposed action be on a small scale. In an audience with the King, the British Prime Minister Lord Balfour expressed the fear that the viceroy was cherishing plans of territorial expansion and that this would damage Indian interests and the empire's international relations.

Although Curzon secured authorization for his plans he managed to antagonize several leading figures in the government in the process: thereafter his influence began to decline. London's reluctance to approve the Indian government's Tibetan enterprise was explained by considerations of its China policy. By contrast Curzon and his senior colleagues were guided by narrower considerations: they saw before them a weak country which could easily be turned into a colony and longed to achieve this aim. The Younghusband expedition is therefore to be seen as an initiative of British India rather than of Great Britain itself. As will be seen, this distinction was to have a significant impact on the outcome of the expedition and the Lhasa convention which concluded it.

The *Times of Ceylon* newspaper clearly expressed its conception of the Anglo-Chinese position. It commented that it was well known that Russia was strengthening its position and influence in Tibet.[5] The present action was necessary to prevent future complications. Russia was paving the way to Tibet by sending numerous scientific expeditions to the northern part of the country. It was time to bring this game to an end.

Curzon made sure that such newspaper reports were taken at face value. He wrote to London that a Chinese customs officer, one of the representatives at the negotiations in Khamba Dzong, had informed Younghusband that he had every reason to believe that the Russians had been on their way to Lhasa. This information had recently been confirmed by the Reuters news agency: several hundred Cossacks had been sent to Tibet.[6]

London understood very well the purpose of such information. However, owing to Curzon's insistence, it decided to sanction Younghusband's move to the Chumbi valley in Tibet. Lord Lansdowne, the foreign minister, explained this move to Count Benckendorff, the Russian ambassador, by claiming that the government had been obliged to take this step because of the Tibetans' scandalous behavior.

Dorjiev's earlier efforts to arouse the Russian government's interest in the Tibetan problem had not borne fruit, and St Petersburg reacted indifferently to reports of Younghusband's advance on Tibetan territory. Lord Hardinge, the deputy secretary of state for India and future viceroy, was in St Petersburg at the time and he reported back to London about his conversation with Lamsdorff. According to Hardinge, Lamsdorff assured him that the Russian government had paid no attention to newspaper reports about an agreement between Tibet and Russia.[7] He referred to the Tibetan mission to Yalta and gave assurances that no political questions between Russia and Tibet had been discussed: there were only religious links between them because of the presence of a large number of Russian Buryats who considered the Dalai Lama to be the highest religious authority. Hardinge pointed out that the mission from Tibet to Russia and Dorjiev's influence in Lhasa was suspicious but said that His Majesty's government accepted with satisfaction Count Benckendorff's official protestations on April 8, 1903 that the Russian government had not concluded any agreements concerning Tibet either with China or Tibet itself. The Russian government had no agents there and had no intention of sending agents or a mission to Lhasa.

Meanwhile, Klem (the Russian consul in Bombay) wrote:

> Judging by Calcutta's indifferent attitude to Tibetan isolation and by the few efforts made in earlier decades to enter into relations with it, one can hardly imagine that the question of adding this country to the British sphere of influence was projected at the convention of 1890. The present viceroy was at first rather reluctant and almost shook his reputation as a vehement supporter of a 'forward policy'. But when the disreputable war (in South Africa) had been finished, England with magnificent speed and cunning again assumed the role of the 'ruler of destinies'.

Although the Russian consul's letter is critical of England, these criticisms did not have a concrete impact on practical politics and the British began their Tibetan project without fear of interference from Russia. At no time did the Russian government act to prevent British action in Tibet.

General-Adjutant Alekseyev, the deputy in the Russian Far East, wired to the Russian legation in Peking in December 1903: "Only direct influence on England in one of its sensitive points in its Asian possessions could prevent the capture of Tibet on which all the Buddhist population of Siberia and Mongolia depends as regards their spiritual life."[8] However, Alekseyev could not himself identify any 'sensitive points' since in practice Russian diplomacy had never used such methods in connection with Tibet, and nothing came of this suggestion.

The invasion of Tibet was not on a large scale. Younghusband, the political head of the mission, was accompanied by an armed detachment led by Brigadier-General James MacDonald. This consisted of a mountain battery with seven guns, a machine-gun subdivision, two guns from the Gurkha units and half a company of field engineers. The sub-divisions consisted of eight Sikh and six Gurkha companies. The whole combatant detachment amounted to some 3,000. In addition there was a field hospital, a field engineer team, transport, communication and cartography sub-divisions. The expedition used local yaks, ponies, mules, bullocks and camels for transport purposes, and several thousand male and female porters were hired to carry heavy loads.

Thus, the total number of people accompanying Younghusband amounted to some 8,000 people. However, it was feared that the Tibetans would offer armed resistance and that military operations would then be inevitable: in that case the guns were to be decisive.

General Macdonald was not an experienced commander, but the situation required neither a large number of soldiers nor great military skill since British military training and weapons gave them overwhelming military superiority over the Tibetans.

The first armed clash took place north of Tuna near Guru on March 31, 1904. On one side were 100 British troops and 1,200 Indians and on the other a large number of Tibetans whose camp was near Guru. The Tibetans were almost unarmed and besides were unfamiliar with modern warfare: they found themselves all but defenceless before the firing of the British soldiers. "That was not a battle but carnage, not a doughty·struggle but massacre," wrote Edmund Candler, a British journalist who accompanied the mission. More than 600 Tibetans were killed and only two British troops were wounded. Public opinion around the world and in England itself responded to news of this 'battle' with indignation.

Younghusband himself acknowledged that the Tibetans had been treated cruelly, but claimed that the collision was inevitable. According to him, the Tibetans 'miscalculated' and 'underestimated' the inflexibility of the British. Indeed, the Tibetans both miscalculated and underestimated, but they were scarcely responsible for the scale of the killing. Long before the 'battle', Lord Hamilton had expressed the view that it would be necessary to kill a few hundred Tibetans to restore British prestige and Candler later wrote that one could not expect the British to be recognised as a great power unless several hundred Tibetans were killed.[9] Thus the mass murder of the Tibetans was the result not so much of their miscalculation but rather the consequence of a planned strategy designed to intimidate them.

However, the butchery at Guru did not frighten the Tibetans. Ten days later the British again came into collision with them. This time about 200 Tibetans were killed on the battlefield and the rest were scattered. The British did not pursue those who fled because there was no time. Thus, as it turned out, neither Tibetan armed opposition nor Russian diplomatic protests impeded Younghusband's advance.

The assertions made by Benckendorff, the Russian ambassador in London, that Russia had no intention of changing the status of Tibet obliged Great Britain to make a similar pledge. In late June 1904, the British foreign secretary assured Benckendorff that the British government would not make any territorial acquisitions in Tibet. The two powers reached a verbal agreement to this effect.

The Russian foreign affairs ministry showed a marked lack of initiative just as it had in previous decades when Russia's highest military and diplomatic officials (Blarambeerg, Skobolev, Ignatiev and others) had sent reports and memoranda proposing to take advantage of England's difficulties in Asia to tame it in Europe. These memoranda had been filed and the government had not taken up the proposals. This lack of initiative is hard to understand. Russia had no interests in Tibet; Dorjiev was dispensable; and the Dalai Lama's letters were left unanswered. But, given that both parties had yet to cool down after their 19th century rivalry in Asia, why should Russia not exploit the Tibetan expedition in its relations with England? One possible explanation for this disinterestedness was the high moral stance of Russian diplomacy. But who would believe this? It has become a custom to defame and revile this diplomacy. Whatever the reason, Russia remained indifferent to Tibet.

Younghusband later reported to his superiors that the rumors about the treaty between China and Russia on Tibet had not been confirmed, though he allegedly had seen a draft of the treaty according to which the Russians had promised to send military instructors to Tibet. The Ch'ing amban informed Younghusband that the Russians had sent rifles to the Tibetans, but these had become so rusty by the time they reached Lhasa that they could not be used. However, Younghusband added that he had not seen those rifles himself.[10]

The fuss about the 'Russian menace' in Tibet was created not only by Curzon but also by the press. L. A. Waddell's book *Lhasa and its Mysteries* appeared the year after the mission. The well-known orientalist S. Oldenburg reviewed the book in the magazine of the Russian public education ministry in September 1905 and pointed out that from a political point of view the main feature of the book was its extreme Russophobia. For example, he repeats the legend that Russia had sent Tibet plenty of arms.[11] Waddell turns G.Ts. Tsibikov into a topographical spy. In fact Tsibikov had been sent by the Russian Geographical Society to carry out scientific research. He did not make any surveys and even avoided learning how to do them so as to avoid trouble.

In his review of events in Tibet, Oldenburg pointed out that the Indian government's eloquence had persuaded London to take undertake aggression in Tibet. Now that the mission was over, it could be stated definitely that the story of Russia sending masses of arms to Tibet was no more than a legend. The only such weapons in the country were a few rifles which had been acquired from Mongols and Buryats. Oldenburg undoubtedly underestimated the durability of the legends concerning Russian intrigue, which persist to this day.

Chapter Four

The Lhasa Convention

Although the Dalai Lama was the banner of resistance, he did not himself take part in the defence of Tibet. In his memoirs, Dorjiev explains quite definitely that the Tibetan councils favored armed resistance. He himself considered that the British were far more powerful than the Tibetans and that the latter should therefore avoid conflict. Dorjiev's pacifist arguments did not convince his opponents. According to him, Tibetan statesmen showed ill-considered narrow-mindedness in questions of war, peace and the salvation of their country. Dorjiev therefore almost single-handedly had to transport animals for the Dalai Lama's escape .

The Dalai Lama realized that Dorjiev's missions to Russia had aroused the suspicions of the British government. Just before escaping from Lhasa he wrote a letter to the British saying that they had no grounds for concern. However, he received no reply because the British military/political machinery was already gathering momentum with a view to achieving its objectives by force rather than diplomacy. Dorjiev was summoned to the Dalai Lama's residence at the Potala, and he and some members of the Dalai Lama's retinue set out to the north-east in the direction of Mongolia. An escort of 200 horsemen soon joined them.

As Younghusband approached Lhasa, the amban sent messengers to the Dalai Lama calling on him to return to Lhasa where he would be treated with respect and courtesy. However, the Dalai Lama foresaw what would happen if he did so, and continued his escape to Mongolia. Having failed to persuade the Dalai Lama to turn back, the amban tried to win over the Tibetan dignitaries who had remained in Lhasa. In a report to the Chinese foreign ministry he expressed his own view that it would be to Peking's advantage if the Tibetans suffered another defeat.[1] He nurtured the idea of taking advantage of British military power to strengthen the power of the ambans in Lhasa and believed that Younghusband's mission would help achieve this.

The Tibetans were aware of the amban's wish to punish them, and reacted accordingly. Perceval Landon, a journalist who accompanied the British expedition, wrote that the Chinese had no real power and that the Tibetans deeply distrusted them, regarding even their advice as a form of poison.[2]

Younghusband's Anglo-Indian force entered Lhasa on August 4, 1904, having travelled nearly 600 km from the Sikkim border with interludes in Khamba Dzong, Tuna, and Gyantse. He established his military headquarters in the suburbs of Lhasa. The amban hastened to make contact with him, and arranged an official meeting a few hours after his arrival. He was preceded by an escort of forty retainers in picturesque dress and carrying pikes, tridents and banners. They were followed by his secretaries and their servants and finally by 10 men carrying the amban himself in a palanquin. The description of the amban's procession on his 'state visit' is significant because it demonstrates the importance he attached to correct protocol, an attitude shared by Younghusband himself.

Younghusband returned the amban's visit the following day, and indicated that Curzon wished to establish a British representative in Lhasa accompanied by a military escort. The amban as usual referred to the foolishness of the Tibetans, and was obviously concerned about his own status. In spite of the weakness of his position he promised to render Younghusband all possible assistance to persuade the Tibetans of the urgent need to settle the problem with the British as soon as possible. In addition, he assigned a two-day food allowance to Younghusband's troops as a gift and indicated his readiness to feed them in future from his own resources. This was very opportune as the delivery of supplies from India was irregular. The Dalai Lama wrote to the Manchu Empress Dowager from exile and blamed the amban for 'various derelictions' which resulted in the British invasion of Tibet.[3]

The Tibetans faced political and military defeat. The Tibetan leaders' meeting with Younghusband was particularly humiliating when compared with the solemn ceremonies which had accompanied the amban's meeting with Younghusband. Urgyan Wangchuk, the Penlop of Tongsa (Bhutan), had accompanied the mission as a mediator, and he introduced them to the British. At the first meeting they were treated more as trophies put out for show rather than as a government representatives authorised to negotiate on a basis of equality.

Before fleeing from Lhasa, the Dalai Lama had appointed the Ti-Rinpoche, the head of Ganden monastery, as the regent, and had given him one of his Great Seals used to ratify religious documents. Younghusband negotiated with him and with the representatives of the three great monasteries of Sera, Drepung and Ganden. The Ti-Rinpoche duly ratified the Lhasa convention, which resulted from these negotiations, with the Dalai Lama's official seal. In the later Chinese view, this amounted to a shameful capitulation to the enemy at the walls of the capital, but the Chinese representative in the capital was to be blamed for this disaster. Not only had he helped Younghusband with food: more importantly he had promoted the Lhasa convention. The Ch'ing government approved of his actions although the Dalai Lama, who was now in Urga (the capital of Mongolia), accused the amban of cowardice and betrayal.

The Lhasa convention consisted of 10 articles, and these reflected the maximum demands which Curzon could inflict on Tibet without coming into conflict with his own government in London. The first articles of the document referred to the original purpose of the expedition, but the subsequent clauses were more significant. They reflected Curzon's view that the official purpose of the mission was insignificant, and the main purpose was to define future relations as a whole rather than the frontier disagreements or conditions for trade. The most important item in the convention was Article Nine. This read:

> The government of Tibet engages that, without the previous consent of the British government:
>
> a) no portion of Tibet shall be ceded, sold, leased, mortgaged or otherwise given for occupation to any foreign power;
> b) no such power shall be permitted to intervene in Tibetan affairs;
> c) no representatives or agents of any foreign power shall be admitted to Tibet;
> d) no concessions for railways, roads, telegraphs, mining or other rights shall be granted to any foreign power. In the event of consent to such concessions being granted, similar or equivalent concessions shall be granted to the British government;
> e) no Tibetan revenues, whether in cash or in kind, shall be pledged or assigned to any foreign power or the subject of any foreign power.

There is no reason to cast doubt on the authority of the Tibetan signatories to the convention. The Tibetan leaders were compelled to negotiate but neither the Chinese nor their own compatriots questioned their authority to do so. In addition to the Great Seal of the Dalai Lama, the seals of the three great monasteries, the council, and the national assembly were attached to the convention. Younghusband had little conception of the role of these institutions in ratifying state resolutions or treaties. It therefore follows that the decision to attach their seals, thus ensuring the validity of the convention, was taken on the initiative of the Tibetans rather than the British.

By signing the convention, the Tibetans achieved their immediate objective of ensuring Younghusband's withdrawal to India. At the same time, the fact that they signed an international treaty in their own right demonstrated Tibet's independent legal status. Tibet had signed similar bilateral agreements in the past, for example in 1842 following a war with the Dogras and in 1856 after a war with Nepal. Chinese historians also were conscious of this aspect of the convention: by his actions the Chinese representative in Lhasa apparently had recognised Tibet's right to conclude international agreements.

Although the Younghusband expedition resulted in Tibet's military and political defeat, the British did not establish any form of colonial power in the country. When signing the convention, Younghusband pointed out that the British had not taken possession of any part of Tibet, and recognised China's suzerainty. The actual results of the expedition were not commensurate with the efforts made in undertaking it. In great measure this was due to the contrasting perspectives and objectives of the Indian government led by Curzon and the British government in London. Younghusband signed the convention in his capacity as the representative of His Majesty's government. Later, on November 11, 1904, it was ratified by Lord Ampthill, the acting viceroy of India during Curzon's furlough, and that was all. It was not formally ratified by the British government in London.

The Tibetan policy of Curzon and Younghusband had in fact gone beyond London's official instructions, and this naturally antagonized the home government. After Younghusband's return to India in October 1904, he disappeared from the Tibetan policy-making arena—as did Curzon himself a little later. The two men's forward policy was not so much a result of indiscipline as extreme zeal. The men on the spot felt that they knew better than their superiors in London. Ten years later there were similar conflicts of opinion concerning the Simla conference between British India,

Tibet and China. In both cases the British government in Whitehall decided not to take full advantage of the benefits secured by the negotiators because these contradicted London's policy towards China.

Soon the Ch'ing government suggested a continuation of Chinese/British negotiations. Sir Ernest Satow, the British minister, was given to understand that the representatives of other western powers in Peking were concerned about the implications of Article Nine, and hoped that they would serve to justify their own claims to special status in certain parts of China: Germany in Shandung; Japan in Fujian; and France in Yunnan. At the same time Peking proposed to pay the indemnity imposed on Tibet. The English at first resisted this proposal because they feared that the Tibetans would ignore the other terms of the convention if Britain chose to deal directly with China on the indemnity. As *The Times* of London wrote, the indemnity was in part a punishment and in part a means of making the Tibetans understand the need to fulfil their other obligations under the Lhasa convention.[4]

However, China did finally pay the indemnity as a means of strengthening Manchu authority in Tibet.[5] Soon the Ch'ing government began to take advantage of this to carry out a more energetic policy of consolidating its influence in Tibet.[6] Having received the financial compensation for Younghusband's mission, the government of British India was inclined to reconcile itself to its failure.

In addition to paying the contribution, the Ch'ing government took other steps to regulate Anglo-Chinese relations concerning Tibet. The delegate Tan Shaoi was appointed to the negotiations concerning the Lhasa convention. In his conversations with Satow, he displayed complete understanding of British concerns. Referring to the 'Russian menace', Tan Shaoi informed Satow that not long after the signing of the 1890 convention, the Dalai Lama had obtained written assurance from Russia of her readiness to protect Tibet against India. These documents, three in number, had been obtained by the Amban Shen Tai, but at some time during the stay of the latter, his subordinates had been bribed to give them up, and subsequently it was found that they had disappeared.[7] Though Satow was not inclined to believe this fascinating information, he nevertheless thought it appropriate to inform London.

Meanwhile, Dorjiev arrived in China en route to St Petersburg. In his statement to the Trans-Baikal military governor, he wrote that the Dalai Lama cherished hopes of Russian assistance to settle the Tibetan question in favor of the Tibetan people, and this was the reason for his journey from Tibet to Urga (Mongolia), which was in the Russians' sphere of influence. However, the Dalai Lama was uncertain of Russia's attitude to the Tibetan question and had therefore entrusted him to travel to St Petersburg to clarify the situation. At the same time an official from Troitskosavsk wired to St Petersburg that the Dalai Lama dreamt of linking Tibet and Russia by telegraph, and that meanwhile he was appointing Dorjiev to be his representative in Russia to inform the Russian government of Tibetan affairs and to receive information from the Russian government.

In St Petersburg, Dorjiev presented an official document, entitled "Reasons for appointing the Ambassador Tsanit Hambo Labsan Agwan, an official of the Dalai Lama, the head of the Tibetan people." The document included the following:

> We ask Your Majesty to take measures to make the Tibetan state inviolable, and prevent the British government from encroaching on Tibet. The Tibetan state has until now been running its affairs independently and henceforth no one will have to interfere with the internal affairs of the state. Having the wish to join the circle of the civilized great peoples, we entrust the above Tsanit Hambo to achieve all kinds of agreements.[8]

However, Dorjiev's negotiations in St Petersburg were fruitless. A "Memorandum on the Negotiations with Hambo Dorjiev" on September 25, 1905 summarized the Russian government's reply to Dorjiev's proposal to renew Russia's connections with Tibet and appoint an official representative to Lhasa: it was thought this would actually harm the Dalai Lama because he would be seen as a Russian protégé.[9]

Nevertheless, academic opinion still disagrees on the subject of Russian pressure on England in connection with the Tibetan crisis. Given Russia's evident indifference towards Tibet during the negotiations with Dorjiev, one cannot agree that Britain's invasion of Tibet and the conclusion of the Lhasa convention caused the resistance of the Russian government. The following diplomatic exchanges cited in one of the Russian works on the period can scarcely be considered examples of Russian pressure: "Sazonov, the chargé d'affaires, declared in London that the text of the treaty had produced an unfavorable impression on the Russian government," or, "The ambassador Benckendorff had a conversation with Lansdowne and pointed out that the treaty amounted to a disguised protectorate," or, least of all, "Lamsdorff, the foreign affairs minister of Russia, set forth his opinion of the Tibetan question to the British ambassador."[10]

After the Lhasa convention was published in the press, the Russian foreign affairs minister wired to the Russian embassy in London:

> The text of the Anglo-Tibetan Treaty confirms that the English have violated their commitments according to the [English] memorandum of May 20 of this year. Please convey this point to Lord Landowne.[11]

The ambassador was to 'convey this point' and no more. In his reply from London, Sazonov answered that during his conversation with Lansdowne, the British minister denied the justness of Russia's objections and could not see any disparity between Britain's promises and the conditions of the convention.[12]

Similarly, in Peking the Russian ambassador Lessar wrote at the end of September, 1904: "I made it clear that England could not act in Tibet as she liked. We are busy in other regions, but if China is resolute it will turn out that she is not alone." However, China was not resolute. Besides, the British ambassador in Peking tried to calm down Vaivuba (from the Chinese ministry of foreign affairs), saying that the convention was a preliminary agreement and that the final one would be discussed in Peking. The Ch'ing government's position influenced the response of other countries: none responded and two months later Lessar informed St Petersburg that "the newspaper rumors about the protests of Germany, Italy and America against the Tibetan agreement were baseless."[13]

The idea of the Russian pressure on Great Britain to annul the Lhasa convention therefore cannot be proved. In theory, Russia might also have had economic motives for protesting about British action in Tibet: it might have wished to prevent Britain taking possession of Tibetan wealth. However, Tibet was not another India famous for its precious stones. In earlier decades Russian travellers had with great difficulty travelled across Tibet and realized that the country was Alpine, had no forests and little topsoil and was thinly populated: there was no proof of rumors about gold and rare minerals in the country. British specialists who had been able to reconnoitre different parts of the country during Younghusband's expedition gave similar reports.[14] The 'mine workings' mentioned in the Lhasa convention were never realized. In short, Russia would have had no economic motive to protest about British expansion in Tibet.

One might also suggest that the Russian monarchy might have felt a sense of common interest with the Ch'ing dynasty. However, the Ch'ing were obstinate, refractory neighbors, and Tsarist diplomacy had little incentive to work in their favor. Moreover, the House of Romanov had closer dynastic links with Britain than with China: King Edward VII was a blood relative of the Russian Emperor Nicholas II.

The most important dynastic relations in the present context are those between China and Tibet. Relations between Imperial China and Tibet were founded on the 'priest/patron' formula. It has become a commonplace to assert that the links between the two countries were based on the personal interdependence of the emperor and the Dalai Lama. But Tibet was not an organic part of China from the cultural, economic and administrative points of view. Despite this inter-relationship, modern publications referring to events at the beginning of the 20th century invariably refer to 'Chinese interests' in Tibet, without mentioning Tibet's interests in China.

There is one final reason to suppose that Russia might have put pressure on Great Britain to give up the Lhasa convention: Tsarist Russia's eastern policy. However, Russian expansion into Tibet would have contradicted common sense: the acquisition of territory in Asia was not an end in itself for Russia since it did not wish to over-extend its forces.[15] Russian travellers at the end of the 19th century had become acquainted with the vast uninhabited regions of Tibet and these were scarcely attractive for expansion.

However, these considerations did not make Russia indifferent to the Tibetan problem. The Younghusband expedition and the Lhasa convention could not escape the notice of the Russian government, which brought its views to the attention to the British government moderately and clearly. Nevertheless, the Russian government's response does not justify describing it as a display of Anglo-Russian rivalry. London would no doubt have preferred to hear praise of the British invasion of Tibet, but it could not expect international approval of its actions designed to obtain one-sided profits. It was well-known that even the London government did not approve of the actions of the British Indian administration. As the Russian Consul Klemm wrote from Bombay: "Curzon's shady enterprise was strictly condemned by Liberals in parliament."[16] The Russian government understood this and instructed its staff working abroad accordingly. As a telegram to the consul in Urga stated: "The mission to Tibet was planned and carried out by the Indian government, regardless of the wishes of the London parliament which openly reproached Lord Curzon."[17]

Thus, the reaction of Russia can be considered natural and restrained and contained no elements of pressure. Russia's position was not indifferent: it was passive. During this period the Tsarist government was involved in the Russian-Japanese war and suppressing the revolutionary movement in its own country: it was scarcely surprising that it had no reserves of energy to influence events in Tibet.

Chapter Five

The Dalai Lama's escape to Mongolia

The Dalai Lama escaped to Mongolia intending to wait for better times in Tibet. He sent Dorjiev to St Petersburg to persuade Russia to help Tibet. In St Petersburg Dorjiev explained the reasons for the Dalai Lama's flight from Lhasa in a number of meetings with the Tsar and his ministers. He later wrote in his autobiography that the Russians had promised help, but that the government had been downcast by its defeat in the war with Japan. Nevertheless, Dorjiev was promised that Russia would render all possible assistance by means of negotiations with the English and the Chinese.

The Russian government made no attempt to influence Tibetan affairs, and this impelled Russian Buddhists to take action on their own account. The Russian consul in Urga wrote that Khambo Lama Iroltuyev, the head of the Russian Buddhists, proposed to take the Dalai Lama to Selenginsk with a view to creating a new Buddhist centre under his leadership. Economic considerations played a role here in that the money spent by pilgrims travelling to see the Dalai Lama would have remained in Russia, instead of being used up in Tibet, if the new Buddhist centre had been established.

While the Dalai Lama was in Urga, Iroltuyev and other influential Buryats and Kalmyks tried to persuade him to come to their country and in this connection he enquired of the Russian consul in Mongolia whether the Russian government could ensure Tibet's protection from England and China. However, he received a negative reply.[1] The Russian government wished to avoid becoming embroiled in Tibetan affairs and the foreign minister instructed the consul to pass over in silence the possibility of a rapprochement between Russia and Tibet.[2] The Dalai Lama learnt of Russia's internal and external problems, and decided that he did not wish to add to its difficulties by entering the country.[3]

The official Chinese chronicle of these events was compiled between 1911 and the 1920s, at a time when the Tibetans did not permit Chinese representatives onto their territory. This explains the aloofness with which the Chinese chroniclers depicted events in Tibet:

> When the English began to advance easily into Tibet, the Dalai Lama was very frightened. Having given his seal to the Kalon [minister] of Ganden monastery, he hurried to escape to Qinghai. The Amban Yu Tai demanded that the Dalai Lama be deprived of his rank and removed from his post since he showed an exceptional rebelliousness and hid himself.[4]

Yu Tai's demands reflected the views of the Ch'ing dynasty and its officials of the Anglo-Tibetan conflict. *Ch'ing-shi Kao* states:

> In the 30th year of Guans'ui [1904], the Dalai Lama was involved in a war with the English. Having suffered a defeat, he escaped and settled down in Urga. He intended to seek refuge in Russia.[5]

The Manchu court declared the Dalai Lama's dethronement for failing in his duties. This action was invalid since the Dalai Lamas were divine by birth, and no power could either elevate a Dalai Lama to the throne or dethrone him. The dethronement therefore had no practical consequences. Thus, the Chinese official documents confirm that the Dalai Lama could expect no sympathy or assistance from the Ch'ings in his struggle against foreign invasion.

Dorjiev's earlier missions to Russia had not resulted in the establishment of Tibetan/Russian diplomatic relations, but the idea of such links had not been abandoned. Dorjiev was not the only one who was anxious to revive the idea, but his views were particularly significant since he belonged to the retinue of the Dalai Lama. As an exile first in 1904 and later in 1910 (after fleeing to India to escape from the Chinese general Chao Erh-feng), the Dalai Lama corresponded with the Russian authorities through Dorjiev. Dorjiev accompanied the Dalai Lama into exile on the first occasion, but not on the second because he was afraid of falling into the hands of the British.

However, even after being separated from Dorjiev, the Dalai Lama did not give up the idea of rapprochement with Russia. In early June, 1905 Pokotilov, the Russian ambassador to China, received Dorjiev (whom he had met earlier in Peking) in Kiachta on the Russian-Chinese border while on his way from Russia. In his report, Pokotilov wrote:

> According to Dorjiev, the main and almost the only reason for the Dalai Lama's coming to Urga was his intention to

> seek Russian protection since misfortunes had befallen Tibet.[6]

At the same time, the Dalai Lama had not given up hope of persuading the Ch'ings to protect Tibet. This seemed especially feasible during the initial period of the Dalai Lama's stay in Urga. At that time, the Russian consul in Urga reported:

> The Dalai Lama intended to ask our ambassador [in Peking] to facilitate his reconciliation with the Chinese government. If Ambassador Pokotilov could influence the Chinese ministers favorably, the Dalai Lama could return to Lhasa.[7]

However, by the time Pokotilov came from Kiachta to Urga, the distance between the Tibetan and Chinese points of view had grown to such an extent that there was little hope of a rapprochement. Pokotilov's conversation almost repeated Dorjiev's words in Kiachta concerning the desirability of a Russian protectorate. However, the decisive factor in Tibet's relationship with China was not the wishes of the Dalai Lama but the Chinese government's failure to look after Tibet's vital interests.

Since Dorjiev's earlier mission to St Petersburg, the Dalai Lama's intentions had been well known to Russian diplomats. The Russian consul in Urga reported that the Dalai Lama had come to Urga with the sole aim of availing himself of Russian advice and assistance. In Urga he found out about a secret instruction which had been sent from Peking to all the border chiefs ordering them to arrest the Dalai Lama if he appeared on the Russian frontier and bring him to the town of Bin-fa-tsian (Bin-fa-tsian is unknown, and it was later thought that the name might stand for 'immediate execution'). The Peking government was sure that the Dalai Lama was heading for Russia.[8] Obviously such a move would have incurred considerable personal risks for the Dalai Lama, and the Russian embassy warned that it would be disastrous for him if the Chinese discovered "our wish to avail ourselves of his services".[9]

The consul in Urga, who was in constant communication with the Russian ambassador in Peking, wrote in 1905: "Placing himself trustingly under the patronage of the Sovereign [i.e. the Tsar], the Dalai Lama would like to know whether Russia could protect Tibet openly from England and China." The ambassador replied: "It is absolutely impossible to give the assurances required by the Dalai Lama." At the same time he advised the consul to assure the Dalai

Lama that he would be cordially received if he came to Russia. However, he would receive no more than private assistance.[10] Count N.P. Ignatiev, one of the leading supporters of Russia's Asian policy, pointed out in a memorandum to the government that the Dalai Lama's escape might have consequences of great importance to Russia. Ignatiev wrote:

> Apparently, he [the Dalai Lama] counted on direct, active Russian support to Tibet, and even on joining Tibet to the Russian state. It is rumored that some other lamas also intended to come from Tibet to Urga, or settle near the Russian border with the hope of approaching our Kalmyks and Buryats.[11]

However, neither Dorjiev's negotiations in St Petersburg nor the Dalai Lama's personal diplomacy prompted Russia to take any action. The Russian government's attitude to the Tibetan problem was invariably reserved. For example, in April, 1905, when the Russian newspaper *Rassvet* published an article entitled "The Wanderings of the Dalai Lama", the foreign ministry wrote to the editorial board. It said that the article had made quite groundless hints that the foreign minister had earlier given the Dalai Lama several assurances but now refused to give him any support when he had to leave Tibet and ask for Russian help.

It added: "As you are aware, the facts absolutely do not correspond to the statements in the newspaper. It was not the foreign affairs ministry but Count Ukhtomskiy who petitioned for the Tibetan deputation in Russia in 1900, thus reassuring them with some unrealizable promises."[12]

Thus, from the moment of his arrival in Urga, the Dalai Lama persistently sought Russian assistance, either personally or through his representatives. Younghusband's expedition was intended to prevent the Dalai Lama from making advances to Russia,[13] but it had the opposite effect. It was difficult for the Dalai Lama to communicate with Russia from Lhasa (via India, the Near East, the Mediterranean and the Black Sea), but much easier to do so from Urga. However, J. P. Shishmaryov, the Russian consul in Urga, wrote:

> It is not very convenient for us to communicate with the Dalai Lama at present. This might harm affairs with China and Mongolia and cast a shadow on our relations with the Chinese Imperial government which disapproves of the Dalai

> Lama travelling to Urga and suspects him of seeking Russian patronage or even crossing the border into Russia. The Dalai Lama must not be allowed to enter Russian territory.[14]

In January 1905, Alexeyev, a deputy-governor in the Far East, received a message from his subordinates in Russia saying that:

> The Dalai Lama intended to go to Russia. He felt offended that he had been met in Urga not by the Russian consul, but only by the secretary of the consulate, and that the consul had communicated with him only by the secretary. He asks whether the government will find it possible to appoint a special Russian official through whom he, the Dalai Lama, may negotiate.[15]

However, the Russian government declined to appoint a representative to the Dalai Lama pleading, as usual, that it was preoccupied with the war with Japan. Thus, the 'Russian menace in Tibet' with which Curzon had frightened the London government, and the 'Russian intrigues and plots' turned out to be a fabrication. This fabrication was accepted by the Ch'ings who throughout the Dalai Lama's exile in Mongolia insisted on his leaving Urga for Sining.[16] However, British Prime Minister Lord Balfour and many of his colleagues were far from convinced of the reality of the Russian threat to Tibet. Lord Hamilton, the secretary of state for India, while sympathetic to his friend Curzon's point of view, felt privately that the viceroy was being a 'trifle alarmist'.[17] However, the London government did order the despatch of an armed mission to Tibet. Once Tibet had been suppressed, London intended it to pass under the full control of the Ch'ings which would leave no room for 'Russian intrigue' or Russian pressure'.

The Russian authorities showed respect to the Dalai Lama in his capacity as a senior religious leader, but that was all. In six months his desire to escape to Russia had begun to wane. In mid-June 1905, when receiving the Tsar's gifts, he told Pokotilov that:

> he had arrived in the north in Urga mainly to secure the high patronage of the Russian Tsar. He understood that Russia had many troubles at present besides Tibet, but he nevertheless still hoped that His Majesty would not deny his merciful attention to him. The Dalai Lama personally asked Pokotilov to protect his interests before the Chinese government.[18]

Russian diplomats took measures to protect the Dalai Lama. In his letter to the Dalai Lama, Pokotilov wrote that in his unofficial conversations with Chinese ministers he had "frequently referred to the inappropriate behavior of Yang Chzhi, the Urga amban, towards the Dalai Lama. The ministers had promised to reprimand the amban."[19]

References to the Russian / Japanese war provided Russian diplomats with a simple excuse for avoiding participation in Tibetan affairs. However, even many years later, when the war was long past and the 1905 revolution had been replaced by years of reaction, Russia maintained its former attitude towards Tibet. Despite Dorjiev's renewed efforts to interest the Russian government in Tibetan affairs and the Dalai Lama's calls for assistance, the Russian government again avoided involvement in Tibetan problems. It did not even wish to play the role of go-between. The Dalai Lama hoped that Russia would find Tibet's lawful demands to be just and, together with the other European powers, would discuss and settle its demands. One of the Tibetan appeals stated that Tibet had appealed to its mighty historical neighbour Russia because it was unfamiliar with the laws and traditions of international relations and did not trust any other powers and nations: it considered all other approaches to contradict its national ethos.

The Ch'ings, who had dethroned the Dalai Lama for his decision to resist the British invasion, hoped in this way to get rid of a Tibetan government which was displaying too much independence. This action was incompatible with the Dalai Lama's status and the history of Sino-Tibetan relations, but its consequences adversely affected the fate both of the Dalai Lama and of Tibet as a whole. Only Russian assistance offered the Dalai Lama an opportunity to improve the situation. In October 1905, Kuzminsky, the Russian consul in Urga, wired:

> The Dalai Lama requests the consulate to implore the Russian government to take upon itself the task of formally mediating between him and the Chinese government in case they break off relations.[20]

This breakdown of relations had become a fact. The Dalai Lama had appealed to the Russian representatives, requesting them to report to St Petersburg that the Peking government had violated his rights and the rights of Mongolia. The Chinese opposition intended to overthrow the Manchu dynasty and restore Chinese rule.

However, neither Tibet nor Mongolia had ever been under the dominion of the Chinese (as opposed to the Manchus). Rather, Mongolia had been master of both China and Tibet, and had subsequently submitted to the Manchu dynasty more as an ally than a subordinate. The Dalai Lama and his supporters decided to separate peacefully from China and become an independent state with the assistance and patronage of Russia.[21]

At that time the Ch'ing dynasty faced increasing opposition from revolutionary activity in China itself. In August 1905 Sun Yatsen issued the "Declaration of the United Union" which stated:

> Those whom we call Manchus are descended from the eastern barbarian dynasties who lived beyond the frontier forts. During the Ming dynasty they often violated the borders of our state. Later, taking advantage of disturbances in China, they intruded into its territory, abolished our Chinese state, seized power and turned us, the Hans, into their slaves. They killed millions of rebels. We have been a people without a motherland for 250 years. Now the cruelty and evil deeds of the Manchu powers has exceeded all measure. The army of justice pursues its aim to overthrow the Manchu government and return the Hans to their sovereign powers.[22]

Russia's position remained unchanged even though the Ch'ing throne had been shaken. Official correspondence between Urga and Peking shows that Russian diplomats wanted to keep the Dalai Lama and his retinue from what they believed to be ill-considered and disastrous actions by involving Russia in their affairs. In a letter to Lamsdorff, Pokotilov pointed out that "it is necessary to make the Buddhist chief priest understand that only after his return to Tibet will we have the opportunity to undertake greater activities with regard to the maintenance of Tibetan independence."[23]

Assistance to the Dalai Lama in upholding the independence of Tibet did not become a part of Russian policy either in 1905 or later when the Ch'ings sent a punitive expedition to Tibet. The Russians cherished the illusion that "the Chinese would by no means support their position in Tibet with arms. They would be quite satisfied with an agreement giving them a semblance of suzerainty."[24]

Thus, the Tibetans' hopes of Russian resistance were not realized, and at one of his meetings with Russian representatives in Urga, the Dalai Lama expressed his disappointment. He reproached them for the lack of consistency in the actions of the Russian official bodies—the Urga consulate, the Peking embassy and the St Petersburg military authorities and ministries. All this put him to severe difficulties because he did not know whom to ask for advice or to whom he should entrust these most confidential ideas.25

This situation was the result of extremely weak links between Russia and Tibet. Tibet was not one of the main focuses of Russian policy: it was primarily of scientific interest. The 1906 Conference of Russian Orientalists, in which S. F. Oldenburg, P.K. Kozlov and others took part, stated that:

> Russia has no direct interests in Tibet. We are interested in Tibet first of all because there are many Buddhists among our Russian subjects, and it is advantageous for us to enjoy the favour of their religious leader. At the same time we are interested...in scientific research in Tibet. The services of our travellers and scientists in this field are universally recognised, including by the English. If possible, we should assert the rights of Russian science to pursue these avenues of research.[26]

The Russian state first acquired Buddhist subjects in the 18th century. Buddhism prospered, and the number of monasteries grew. By the early 20th century there were 46 monasteries and 15,000 monks in Buryatia; 105 temples and 5,000 monks in Kalmykia; and 33 temples and about 4,000 monks in Tuva. All this gave Russian academics an opportunity to make direct contact with Buddhism and the study of Tibet.

As far back as the 1830s Isaak Jakob Schmidt of the Russian Academy of Sciences had compiled the first Tibetan-Russian dictionary. Schmidt's Tibetan grammar had appeared in 1839. By the beginning of the 20th century Russia had presented the world with scholars such as V.P. Vasiliev, I.P. Minaev, and F.I. Sherbatsky whose works revolutionized international Buddhist studies.

Unfortunately, Agvan Dorjiev's name is not included in the list of famous scholars although he was the best-educated Tibetologist of all: he left no scholarly works, and even his diaries, which were written in Tibetan, have yet to be translated. He was not writing history: he was creating it.

In short, the thesis that Russia took an active stance in putting pressure on Britain to give up the results achieved by Younghusband's expedition turns out to be quite groundless.

Chapter Six

Curzon's fantasies are put to an end

The world's political scientists and historians have created an enduring myth that Tibet indisputably belongs to China. This myth about the relationship between the two parties has led to a wrong interpretation of the Lhasa Convention of 1904 and the Peking Convention of 1906. The former was, in fact, a denial of any form of Tibetan dependence on China. It completely ignored the Chinese empire. This lack of any mention or implication of the empire reflected the reality of the two states' relationship.

Such disregard, however, seemed inexplicable to the rest of the world because of the notion of these relations that was supported and successfully spread by the Chinese state machinery. Thus the historians' picture emerged that the European states, out of strong rivalry with Britain, began to protest against the Lhasa Convention in order to restore a Chinese presence in Tibet, with China and Russia being in the first ranks of the protesters. China was defending her rights, while Russia was expressing sympathy for China and her rights. As a result of those protests, Britain had to retreat and conclude the Peking Convention with China, re-establishing China's presence in Tibet.

It would be futile, however, to look for any trace of these states' protests. They did not exist, although fictitious stories about them are still repeated in historical articles and in textbooks and lectures for students. Russian diplomatic documents observed that information and rumors about protests on the part of Germany, Italy, America, and about "the particular protests of the Russian government" had proved to be no more than false rumors.1 No one had compelled the London government to renounce the advantages of the Lhasa Convention. Acting precipitously, it had done so on its own initiative.

Writing at that time, Perceval Landon, in whose presence the convention had been signed, noted in his book: "We have acted throughout with the cordial assent and advice of the Wai-wu Pu (the Chinese ministry of foreign affairs), and China has already reaped no small advantage from our vigorous action."[2] Landon's dispassionate voice has not been heard. Present authors seldom manage to appraise the situation soberly and state that Younghusband and Curzon's Tibetan enterprise had met with disapproval from the London government, which almost immediately then reversed its course and made an agreement with China that Great Britain was "to pursue a policy of self-denial in Tibet".[3]

Among the Chinese authors who have supported the "protest" version, the voice of She Su has sounded in discord with the rest of the chorus: "The fate of the Lhasa Convention was nothing like the fantasies of Curzon and other aggressively inclined figures. The primary reason for this was the inner contradictions of British imperialism,"[4] not any kind of protest. Let us also then agree that the convention of 1904 was the result of the viceroy's own initiative, and did not express the better interests of the British empire.

The conclusion of the Lhasa Convention did not conform with the general line of British policy in Tibet and China. The London cabinet, with Balfour at its head, was indignant at the results of Younghusband's expedition. Even the king of Great Britain, who at first had intended to reward "the hero of Lhasa", later had expressed his deep regrets about the fact that Younghusband, in concluding the Lhasa Convention, had acted in "such an extraordinary way...in direct and deliberate defiance of instructions."[5]

This insubordination had nothing to do with an anarchic disregard of state interests. It was caused by the different Tibetan policies of the governments of British India and Great Britain herself. "If Younghusband later strayed from the spirit of his instructions, he could not be wholly blamed, particularly since he knew that Curzon viewed them more as licence to pursue India's destiny as he saw it rather than a rigid and inhibiting blueprint of policy."[6] Having been admonished by Curzon in a certain way, Younghusband merely was doing his best to fulfil the mission with which he had been charged. But London took a different view.[7]

The British government had been seeking to reach an agreement with the Ch'ing government. This found its expression in the bilateral agreement, the Anglo-Chinese Convention of 1906, which appeared as the logical continuation of the "imperialistic deal at the expense of Sikkim" laid down in the previous Anglo-Chinese Convention of 1890. When the Ch'ing government sent its representative Tang Shao-i to Lhasa, it authorized him also to discuss with the British issues concerning the Lhasa Convention.

The failure of the negotiations was quite natural and inevitable. The viceroy's government had been keen to preserve Article

Nine of the convention unchanged, as it gave British India powerful means of influence over Tibet. But this was the very article that affected the Ch'ing authorities, because in it, China was regarded as a foreign state vis-a-vis Tibet. True, immediately after the convention had been signed, Younghusband had hastily reassured that the term "foreign states" in the article did not apply to China. Still, his oral assertions had not been reflected in any official documents and thus could not cast a shadow on the exciting prospects this clause had presented to the colonial authorities of British India.

Article Nine, together with Younghusband's expedition, were the climax of British India's claims on Tibet, although the real capabilities of exercising these claims had not been taken into consideration. Nevertheless, Curzon continued to hold on to it; and Younghusband, for his part, made use of his connections in London to establish personal correspondence with the British king in order to prove that none of his Lhasa achievements for the sake of the Crown should be yielded.

Aware that Great Britain was not about to quarrel with the Chinese empire on account of Tibet, which Britain had suppressed in 1904, the Ch'ing government reversed its Tibet policy. It now planned to take military-political measures, which had become possible due to the recent events in Tibet that British India had initiated, directed and enacted. Within a few months of the conclusion of the Lhasa Convention, it already became known that the Ch'ing authorities intended to proclaim Tibet a province of China. In the bordering Tibetan-populated areas of Batang and Litang, the first punitive expeditions were being prepared under the command of Chinese general Chao Erh-feng, who later gained the reputation of being an executioner of the Tibetan people.

During the negotiations held in Calcutta in March, 1905, Tang Shao-i was already slighting the Lhasa Convention as the "so-called" convention of September 4, 1904. He alleged that the Ch'ing government had nothing to do with it, thus completely ignoring the fact that the amban in Lhasa had closely co-operated with Younghusband at the time of negotiation with the Tibetans. Referring to the Anglo-Chinese agreements of 1890 and 1893, he proposed to settle the Tibetan problem bilaterally, excluding the Tibetans themselves. However, in Calcutta, the powerful "pro-Tibetan" forces in the British India government suppressed these attempts, realizing that Tibetan issues could not possibly be solved without Tibet.

The above-mentioned incongruity of views as well as the strife between the two groups of political figures became vividly apparent during the Calcutta negotiations. Henderson, the British functionary, was included in the membership of the Chinese delegation to the negotiations as Tang Shao-i's counsellor.

Henderson was an officer of the Imperial Naval Customs Service Office, which was directed in its entirety by Britishmen.[8] This was in keeping with a very important feature of British policy in the East, including China, namely that it was to be pursued by professional orientalists with good knowledge of local language, customs, traditions and so forth. The fact that Henderson belonged to this group of British officers in China explains his common view with the British government on their role and tasks. These officers expressed the interests of the British empire. They were dependent on London and suppressed any encroachment upon their rights and status on the part of officials of British India. This confrontation sometimes reached the intensity of conflict.

No wonder that Henderson did not have the slightest sympathy for the British India officials who had disobeyed the directives of London, as was the case with the recent Younghusband mission. Moreover, Henderson considered the Lhasa Convention illegal and spoke about this openly when talking to his Indian partners in negotiations. Of course, he did so not because he wanted to protect the Tibetans, whom he treated no less haughtily than did his Chinese colleagues, but in order to support the position of the latter.

The convention of 1906 was the main consequence of the Anglo-Chinese mutual understanding and not of the "taking into consideration the Russian government's attitude towards the Anglo-Tibetan agreement of 1904." Settling the Tibetan problem through negotiations with the Chinese government and renouncing its Tibetan "gain" acquired so rashly by British India in defiance of London's wishes, will and direct orders, the British government was straightening its general line of relations with the Chinese empire, which the overzealous Lord Curzon had perverted. It also was gaining the Ch'ing authorities' gratitude, since they were now obtaining the possibility to retain a decorum of command over Tibet and so could now prepare to secure their position there with the help of military force. The convention of 1906 had paved the way for the untiring flow of further Ch'ing expansion.

Thus, British intervention in Tibet and the Anglo-Chinese agreements which resulted from it were used by the Ch'ing authorities to consolidate their domination over Tibet. This was at first in its eastern part. As early as 1904, a second amban was appointed in addition to the one in Lhasa. This was to the town of Chamdo.

The Dalai Lama wrote to Dorjiev in Petersburg that "starting from 1904, the Lhasa amban, together with the Chinese military authorities of Szechuan, were regularly committing robberies, mass murders of monks and laymen, destruction of monasteries and similar kinds of excesses in the eastern part of Tibet."[9] The amban in Chamdo likewise treated Buddhist monks quite intolerably. As a result, dissatisfaction with him grew into an implacable hostility. In April, 1905, an uprising broke out and he was killed. This uprising was not merely a local phenomenon. Disturbances had spread to southwestern Szechuan and northwestern Yunnan. Several large monasteries took part in it. Lyuba, the Russian consul general in Urga, was informed about the Tibetan uprising and, while meeting him, the Dalai Lama, "referring to the recently received information from Tibet, told him in detail about the killing of Chinese officials by Tibetans in Kham, the province of eastern Tibet next to Szechuan."[10]

However important this uprising was in its scale and consequences, it was not the first open armed opposition to the Ch'ing authorities' domination in Tibet. According to official Ch'ing documents, during the very first months of the British invasion of Tibet, the Dalai Lama had gathered soldiers from different parts of the country in order to rebuff foreign intervention. After arriving in Lhasa, the most active group of these soldiers had besieged and attacked the amban's residence, and a few dozen of them were killed. This assault marked the beginning of armed action against the Chinese in Tibet, which later took the shape of the national liberation movement.

The uprising in eastern Tibet was suppressed by Ch'ing general Chao Erh-feng, the governor general of Szechuan. In the years that followed, his name became associated with the Manchu Ch'ing repressions, carried out in Tibet on an unprecedented scale. These were furthered, to no little extent, by the 1906 Anglo-Chinese Convention's recognition of the Ch'ing authorities' special rights in Tibet. In the final period of their rule, the Ch'ing authorities started actively to pursue in Tibet the "i-xia bien-i" policy, that is, the policy of "Sinification and adaptation of the barbarians to Chinese ways". They ruthlessly suppressed the Tibetans' aspiration to rid themselves of the Ch'ing's yoke. The persecution of lamaism by the Ch'ing authorities in Tibet caused massive popular revolts, marking the beginning of the struggle against Manchu-Chinese control.

In the eastern part of Tibet, populated by semi-independent Tibetan tribes, Sino-Tibetan conflict had already started at the very beginning of the century. Ch'ing troops, at that time, had set about bowing the people to obedience, doing this, of course, in their own way. The new deputy-amban, Feng Chen, had made a stop in Ba while travelling to his place of appointment in Lhasa. He presumed to make a remark that there were too many monks in the monastery, and that some of them had better return to agriculture. The monks were filled with indignation: a stranger had come to their monastery trying to impose his own regulations. This led to a serious quarrel, and Feng Chen was killed, together with his escort.

Troops from Szechuan under the command of General Ma T'i-t'ai were sent to punish the monks of Ba. The latter had no Tibetan troops nearby to defend them, and so were forced to surrender. The general arrested 322 monks, whom he suspected to be involved in Feng Chen's murder. He had these monks executed, their property confiscated and, at the same time, some monastery buildings burnt down. After this, Ma T'i-t'ai returned to Szechuan.

Soon, however, Chao Erh-feng unexpectedly appeared in Ba under pretence of proceeding with the investigation of Feng Chen's case. He had four more monks put to death, and the monastery heavily fined. Not only opposition, but even the slightest objection to Chao Erh-feng's actions was punished with the death penalty. Mass executions began, and monasteries were razed to the ground. Chao Erh-feng's extremely ruthless repressions stirred up the Tibetans, causing a reciprocal wave of hostility. Many who were lucky enough to survive the 1906 summer suppression of uprisings in Yunnan, Szechuan and Batang gathered at Sang-chi Ling monastery in Hsiang-ch'eng district. This monastery soon became a centre of Tibetan opposition, in which armed nomad forces were also mustered.

Hsiang-ch'eng district is situated in the mountains to the south of the then main road leading from Kanding (Ta-ch'ien-lu) through Litang, Batang and Chamdo proceeding west to Central Tibet. From here, Tibetans raided Chao Erh-feng's lines of communication. Seizing this district thus became a primary objective for his Chinese army. In January, 1906 Chao Erh-feng reached the monastery. His 2,000 soldiers, equipped with German rifles and four cannons which were acquired from Krupp's factories, laid into it. From a military point of view, the monastery was a formidable installation. Its walls were about a meter and a half thick and more than six meters high. It was a strong fortress defended by over 2,000 monks.

Despite managing to cut off all wâter to the defenders, Chao Erh-feng never succeeded in breaking their resistance during this siege that lasted half a year. The Tibetans successfully repelled all attempts to take the fortress, and only a war ruse helped in the end. The besieged opened the gates of the monastery when they saw what appeared to be an advanced detachment of Tibetan troops rushing to their help. But these were adherents of Chao Erh-feng. Thus the defenders of the fortress-monastery had been taken by surprise and were defeated. Almost all of them fell at the hands of the aggressors. The monastery was razed to the ground.

Subduing the eastern districts of Tibet one by one, Chao Erh-feng made his way with fire and sword through the country all the way to Lhasa. His military campaign against Tibet considerably surpassed Younghusband's expedition in its scale and cruelty.

The above episode of the siege of Sang-chi Ling monastery shows that the unco-ordinated, spontaneous revolts of the Tibetans were undermined by disagreements among various groups of Tibetan local rulers. These rulers often followed a pattern of undisguised treachery and never came to the help of these popular revolts.

Being not only a merciless punisher, but an ardent and energetic administrator as well, Chao Erh-feng planned to open schools in Tibet. Because most of the younger generation of Tibetans looked upon the Chinese newcomers with dislike and hostility, he hoped that with the help of secular education, he could wean them away from the influence of monasteries and monks. The continuing exile of the Dalai Lama produced favorable conditions for such innovations. Nevertheless, unparalleled cruelty remained his main way of "pacifying" Tibet, as even his own superiors blamed him a few years later. The system of government he created rested upon the presence of military garrisons.

Tibetan counteraction was unsuccessful because her state leaders themselves had been misdirected. Due to Dorjiev's influence, the Dalai Lama expected Russia to protect Tibet against the Anglo-Chinese onslaught. But this expectation had not been justified; no help was ever rendered. Where were the Tsar's armies when Younghusband approached Lhasa? Where were the Cossacks he needed to convey him back to Lhasa, and why had the agitations of Russian agents failed to rally Tibetan monks in an effective defence of Tibet against the army of Chao Erh-feng?[11]

The Tsar's government would not interfere in Tibetan events. Sven Hedin, an explorer of central Asia, noted that one of the outstanding champions of an active Russian policy in Tibet, Prince Ukhtomskiy, who had a strong influence on the Tsar, had tried to convince him that the Tibetans wished Russia to establish a protectorate over Tibet. But at the time of the events described here, the Russian emperor, who had granted Hedin a prolonged audience, did not have any political aspirations concerning Tibet, although he did have a personal interest in the country. During this talk there were no signs of any influence from Prince Ukhtomskiy who, from the very beginning when Dorjiev had appeared on the political arena, had been suggesting to the autocrat that Russia should turn her face to the East.[12]

Historians have been convinced that the prince had expansionist plans concerning Tibet and the Tibetan lobby around the Tsar. The above-mentioned small piece of information about him contained in Dorjiev's autobiography gave ground for seeing him as a political figure nourishing aggressive intentions. But the truth was quite different. There was nothing threatening about him.

Prince Esper Esperovich Ukhtomskiy, a philosopher and writer of verse, whose head was filled with various Tibetan fantasies, belonged to the court circles of St Petersburg. In 1904, he published a book under the title *From the Land of Lamaism: On the English Campaign in Tibet*, which was written on the occasion of Younghusband's mission.

The book begins with an extremely impressive phrase: "We have been too late! The English are going to invade imperiously the kingdom of the Dalai Lama."[13] Judging by its beginning, the book should be about the political and military struggle of England and Russia for Tibet. But there is not a word about it. It is wholly dedicated, as the title suggests, to the issues of religion, missionary work and, partly, to travels.

He makes only casual mention of the campaign: "What constitutes the main danger of the movement of English troops into the country of `burkhans and lamas'? The monasteries of those places are extremely rich. They are the true breeding ground of an ancient culture, full of highly artistic cultural relics and the most rare literary monuments. If merely sepoys reach Tashilhunpo and Lhasa, undoubtedly they will, being fanatic heretics and, with their passion for robbery so excellently displayed in the days of the recent suppression of the Boxer Rebellion, cruelly smash the most sacred Lamaist sanctuaries... Oriental Studies will suffer endless losses."

In the final part of the book, he writes, "Anyone who has attempted to grasp the historical process of (evolution of) Western travellers' learning about Tibet, must surely consider the level of our (stressed by Ukhtomskiy—N.K.) knowledge and the uncertainty of our purposes with respect to Tibet to be unpardonably miserable..."

And finally, in the concluding phrases of his publication, the sense of his first exclamation is disclosed: "We have been too late with our vaguely implemented aspiration to enter into more intimate intercourse with the kingdom of the Dalai Lama. Russia, while having versatile experts on Buddhism, will now have to receive the most important information about Tibet, which is inclined towards us, from the hands of those who are nearly estranged...England can take hold, territorially, of the lamas' world, but only those who would not lift a destructive hand against Buddhist holy objects will manage to subdue it spiritually and bring it nearer to themselves."

None of the spirit of this semi-poetic essay contains any bellicose intentions or feelings, or intolerance of the events taking place in Tibet. There is no mention of any existing in the closest circles of the Tsar, or of any plans to solve Tibetan problems or any attempts to work out such plans. On the contrary, it states "the uncertainty of purposes with respect to Tibet". This uncertainty of purposes of Russia remained unchanged in the times to come as well.

The exaggerated opinion about the involvement and interests of Russia in Tibetan affairs, the primary source for which was the British diplomatic corps and the press that served it, could not deceive the Chinese government, which was carrying out its measures of military suppression in Tibet without any fears. In the Tibetan districts seized by his troops, Chao Erh-feng began to introduce new regulations. Thus, in Batang district, it was prescribed that:

> "All inhabitants of the Batang area...are now subjects of the Chinese emperor and subject to the jurisdiction of a Chinese magistrate. All taxes are to be paid to the Chinese. All inhabitants...are now subject to Chinese law. In the very near future, a Chinese school is to be opened at Batang for the

instruction of local Tibetans. Each Tibetan family in the Batang area is to select a Chinese surname. The inhabitants of Batang are to dress themselves according to Chinese customs,"[14] and so on.

In Chengdu and other larger towns of Szechuan, proclamations were distributed saying that eastern Tibet was open for Chinese colonisation and that there were fertile soils which Tibetans did not cultivate due to their ignorance. Unmarried Chinese, the proclamations declared, could easily find wives there, since it is known that, while Tibetan men are inveterately lazy, Tibetan women are extremely industrious.

Only a limited number of Chinese peasants, however, responded to the authorities' appeal. This was partly because the fertility of the soils in fact had proved to be rather grossly overstated, and partly because the areas that had been declared to be free of Tibetans in reality appeared to be populated by the native inhabitants. Thus the rigorous climate and inhabitance of the eastern Tibet territory became the obstacles to Chinese colonisation, which Chao Erh-feng never succeeded in overcoming. Nevertheless, the Ch'ing government never lessened its efforts to turn Tibet into a Chinese province, and Chao Erh-feng received ever higher assignments and wider powers.

Chapter Seven

Forward to a cordial consent

Military-diplomatic manoeuvres by the British government and the colonial authorities of British India, which had led to the concluding of the agreements of 1904 and 1906, and which had given the Ch'ing government the possibility that it readily used for establishing its supremacy over Tibet, were now carried out with respect to Russia as well. The Ch'ing policy of turning Tibet into a province and abolishing the ancient theocratic system of state rule and the Dalai Lama's authority touched the sphere of international relations, where the mutual interests of the parties were somehow interlaced. However distant Russia pretended to be from Tibetan events, the British diplomatic corps could not ignore her completely.

The thesis of Anglo-Russian rivalry had become an anachronism by this time, and could not serve, in this case, as a driving force for British diplomacy. Britain therefore aimed to obtain Russian consent to what was happening in Tibet: Russia was to give recognition to Ch'ing China's Tibetan policy. This would guarantee support of British interests not only in Asia, but in Europe as well, since it would make Russia a British ally in the face of the Austro-German coalition.

Long before the signing of the Anglo-Chinese Convention of April 27, 1906, British Minister of Foreign Affairs Grey had negotiated in London for three months with Russian Ambassador Benckendorff. The purpose of these negotiations was to prepare the ground for the conclusion of an Anglo-Russian agreement on Asian issues.

A month after the Anglo-Chinese Convention had been signed, British Ambassador Nicolson arrived in Petersburg to hold talks with the Russian government. In an "entirely private note" of Minister of Foreign Affairs Izvolskiy, dated May 27, 1906, it was reported that "Arthur Nicolson has expressed his readiness to set about discussing first of all Tibetan matters. He has delivered me a text of the recently concluded convention with China, having added that this text might probably not be quite exact, because the original convention had not as yet been received in London."[1]

From the very beginning of negotiations between Nicolson and

Izvolskiy, the Tibetan problem was presented by the British ambassador as being the most important issue in comparison with the forthcoming settlement on Persia and Afghanistan. The following were the main points, as concerned Tibet, of an agreement with Russia that Nicolson was commissioned to obtain:

1. Russia should recognize Chinese suzerainty over Tibet and offer her pledge to respect Tibet's territorial integrity and not interfere in her internal affairs.
2. In accordance with the above-mentioned condition, Russia should acknowledge that, due to her geographic position, Great Britain has special interests that render it necessary that no state disturbs Tibetan foreign affairs.
3. The British and Russian governments oblige themselves not to send their representatives to Lhasa under any circumstances.
4. The British and Russian governments agree not to seek to be granted any concessions for themselves or for their citizens to build roads, railways, mines or any such similar things in Tibet.
5. The British and Russian governments agree that no Tibetan incomes, in goods or currency, be paid or pawned to them or their citizens.

The five clauses of this proposed agreement with Russia constituted a further development of the conditions set in the Lhasa and Peking agreements that Great Britain had formerly signed. Russia was now supposed to give her consent to them. The British and Anglo-Indian governments were struggling, then, in talks with the Russians, to obtain official recognition of the new status quo created by the Anglo-Tibetan and Anglo-Chinese treaties.

The Tsar authorized his minister of foreign affairs to conduct negotiations on the basis of the British draft. Nicolson was informed of this as well. From the very start of negotiations, the Russian party showed no aspirations to gain any advantage in the Tibetan matter. This was actually the only item on the agenda and both sides had no disagreements over it. In a letter from Minister of Foreign Affairs Izvolskiy informing the Russian ambassador to Peking, Pokotilov, about the conditions the British were setting, the only doubts he expressed concerned the second paragraph of these conditions.

Izvolskiy wrote: "I told the British ambassador that, first of all, it was necessary to explain the true meaning of the second clause in the draft. If Great Britain, due to its geographic position, has special interests, then it must be acknowledged that Russia too has certain interests arising from her Buddhist citizens' religious dependence on the head of the Tibetan state. This dependence gives us ground for dealings with the Dalai Lama that do not have any political character and do not constitute any interference with Tibetan internal affairs. Therefore, it is fair to change the wording of the second clause. Besides, the subnote to the clauses must not be an obstacle for organizing Russian scientific expeditions to Tibet."[2] "The subnote to the clauses" reads that Russian officials could not go to Tibet under any circumstances whatsoever.

In his answer, Pokotilov presented his observations on the proposed negotiations: "We could have been satisfied with such a state of affairs (as existed after the conclusion of the Anglo-Chinese Convention of 1906) and, for our own part, not being bound with any obligations towards Tibet, calmly waited for the development of the situation in this country. But, addressing us, the government of Great Britain obviously intends to add our consent...to the clauses of the treaty of the 27th of April (the Anglo-Chinese Convention) and ensure for itself the impossibility of interference on our part into the sphere of Tibetan policy. Seemingly, there are no similar incentives on our part...All our interest displayed towards Tibetan issues in general may be justified only by the observation that any standing we achieve in this respect gives us a possibility, when the moment is right and for a suitable compensation, to give up any further interference in Tibetan affairs, which in itself could hardly ever be of any importance to us."[3]

Pokotilov, as well as Izvolskiy, also noted the inequality implicit in the second clause of the agreement the British party proposed. He wrote that, in his opinion, it could be interpreted "in a sense that is rather unfavorable towards us, and we should avoid such a situation by every means possible." He also expressed here his supposition that it would be possible to use "the Anglophobic tendencies of the high priest (the Dalai Lama), which could be an influential factor in our favor in settling our relations with England in future." However, he suggested that utilization of this factor was to be limited by very narrow frames and be short-term, also adding that "there is hardly any reason to regard the high priest's return to Lhasa as an event that would be favorable from the point of view of active Russian policy in Tibet."[4]

Pokotilov's letter reflected the official Russian view on this situation quite well. It passed through the bureaucratic staircase up to the very top, where the imperial hand inscribed on it: "To my mind, Pokotilov's observations are correct."[5]

Not only the diplomatic department, but also other important state institutions took the same stand. In September, 1906 Armed Forces Chief of Staff Palitsyn, in a letter to Minister of Foreign Affairs Izvolskiy, noted: "In the ranks of the enormous number of extremely vast and complicated issues to be discussed, Tibetan affairs are the least urgent for us, that is to say, they affect our essential interests to the least extent. The Tibetan issue is almost the only one which we, being, so to say, free from English pressure in this case, may use in the course of interchanging interests and concessions...We are not pampered by England's generosity and are rather inclined to believe that, always seeking practical advantage for herself, she will accept our pledges regarding Tibet with pleasure, but will not make any concessions as a result, either in Afghani or Persian matters."[6]

The Russian orientalists Semyonov, Kozlov, Oldenburg and others were asked to express their opinion about the forthcoming Anglo-Russian negotiations. In their recommendations, they stated that "Russia should try to satisfy her interests, which are not so numerous, in a diplomatic manner, because there is no other course of behavior, and we have no opportunity to undertake anything against England. Be that as it may, we are bound with a certain moral obligation with respect to the Dalai Lama and, as such is the case, we cannot help but do all we can to guarantee his personal security and, as far as possible, to maintain his stature and authority. It is precisely this that defines the task we are to accomplish at this moment."[7]

The correspondence of Russian diplomats on the convention of 1907 convinces us once more that neither the Anglo-Chinese convention of 1906, nor the convention of 1907 itself, in its Tibetan part, were the result of notorious "Russian pressure". Their only initiator and almost exclusive compiler and author was the British diplomatic corps. The latter was representing the London government, which acted fearlessly and without taking into account any external pressure, insistence or demands on the part of the government of British India. British diplomats even pointed out to the new viceroy of India, Lord Minto, that Britain could not have two foreign policies. The decision to discuss problems of central Asia with Russia had been taken, and the government of British India was obliged to obey it implicitly: "Be we right or wrong, that is our policy."[8]

The Anglo-Russian Convention of 1907, with its recognition of Chinese suzerain rights over Tibet in its preamble and its subsequent development of this thesis in its contents, brought to nil all Curzon's efforts to "master" Tibet and all the results he had achieved in this respect. Everything that he had cherished and realized while ruling India as its viceroy went to rack and ruin.

British opposition to this convention consisted mainly of high-ranking Indian administrators in London. But Curzon and Younghusband's critical addresses against an "incomprehensible" renunciation of everything that had been reached in Tibet, their stern condemnation of this renunciation, and their characterization of the complete loss of all their Tibetan achievements as a "universal failure", could not shake the government in London.

According to the information of the St Petersburg telegraph agency in London on January 24, 1908, "The debate in the House of Lords on the occasion of the Anglo-Russian agreement was opened by Lord Curzon's speech", who declared, in particular, that "the treaty, in all appearance, is a complete surrender and great humiliation on the part of England." Such a dramatic definition of the step undertaken in no way influenced the listeners, however, because the question had arisen as part of the personal drama of Lord Curzon and his own private policy, not the policy of the British empire.

According to the first clause of the British draft of the agreement on territorial integrity of Tibet and non-interference with its internal affairs, the first article of the convention draft read: "The two high contracting parties agree to respect the territorial integrity of Tibet, and to abstain from all interference in its internal administration."[9] In development of the condition contained in the preamble about the rights of China over Tibet, the second article of the convention established: "In conformity with the admitted principle of the suzerainty of China over Tibet, Great Britain and Russia engage not to enter into negotiations with Tibet except through the intermediary of the Chinese government."[10]

In both cases, when Chinese suzerainty over Tibet is mentioned, the text of the convention differs from that of the British draft. If, in the draft, this suzerainty was set as a reality, the convention speaks only about the right of suzerainty and the principle of suzerainty.

This discrepancy displays the difference in attitude of the two contracting parties. If the British party preferred to consider Chinese suzerainty over Tibet to be an actual fact, its partner, the Russians, recognized merely the right and the principle of such suzerainty. This reflected the true situation and implied the possibility that Tibetan events might develop in another direction, which would be possible in case of stubborn Tibetan resistance to Chao Erh-feng's punitive forces.

The difference in the texts of the draft of the agreement and the convention itself, no doubt, was a consequence of a discrepancy in viewpoint of the contracting parties during the negotiations. The Dalai Lama, who had escaped from Tibet, was in Mongolia, where he maintained extensive contacts with Russian citizens. Furthermore, Russia also took interest in the Dalai Lama and his future destiny, as he was the supreme ruler of Tibet and the head of Buddhism.

The position of the representative of the Russian government at the negotiations, therefore, took into account the Buryat Buddhists who lived in areas on the Russian side of the border between the Russian and Chinese empires. These Russian citizens were important from a military point of view: their fighting ability was of great significance for the Russian armed forces. They considered the Dalai Lama their spiritual head, and it was therefore in the interests of the state not to infringe upon those interrelations.

A tumultuous Anglo-Chinese campaign soon appeared in the press in connection with "The Intrigues of the Thirteenth Dalai Lama with the Tsar", referring to Dorjiev's embassy to Russia. Once more this proved to be insubstantial in the light of Izvolskiy's announcement during the negotiations that his country's relations with Tibet had purely a spiritual character, and that Russia was in no way interested in this particular Dalai Lama. If the English wished to do so, they could change him for another Dalai Lama that would suit them better.[11]

But, for the British party, such substitution of a Dalai Lama would entail a serious interference in Tibetan internal affairs. It would have necessitated asking the Ch'ing government for their help, which they would hardly have rendered, because this Dalai Lama was not an advocate of resistance to Chinese troops in Tibet. In fact, later, after his return to Lhasa, he called for his countrymen to lay down their arms.

The British party had neither proof for refuting Izvolskiy's statement, nor any wish to do so. Even the government of British India, despite being especially sensitive to the "Russian spirit" in Tibet, had no objections to visits of Buryat pilgrims to Lhasa in accordance with the practice of the time. Lack of any reason for seeing pilgrims as political agents was established in the convention by an agreement between the parties that "Buddhists, subjects of Great Britain or of Russia may enter into direct relations on strictly religious grounds with the Dalai Lama and the other representatives of Buddhism in Tibet; the governments of Great Britain and Russia engage, so far as they are concerned, not to allow those relations to infringe upon the stipulations of the present arrangement."[12]

As has been mentioned above, the Dalai Lama's authority was held extremely high in the eyes of Buryat Buddhists, and they were ready to assist his return to Lhasa in every way, even to the extent of rendering him armed protection on his march to his homeland. But this "local incentive", which gave Russia quite a reasonable basis for sending her armed detachment to Tibet as an escort for the Dalai Lama, was also neither approved nor implemented.

Noting a certain passiveness on the part of the Russian diplomatic corps at the negotiations, in that they did not insist on discussing any of the questions raised by Izvolskiy, one can see, at the same time, how intent were the actions of the British diplomats. A special deliberative body was organized under the chairmanship of Izvolskiy to discuss issues concerning the planned convention. The minister of finance, the heads of all military departments and the minister of trade and industry were also included in the membership of this council. It was the supreme collegiate, the body to solve the program issues of the convention. However, the Tibetan sections of the convention were never discussed during the meetings of this special council.

The question about scientific expeditions to Tibet was not reflected in the text of the convention. But, at Nicolson's suggestion, the parties exchanged letters in which they expressed a mutual renunciation of sending expeditions to Tibet during the next three years. On August 18 (31), 1907, the Anglo-Russian Convention on Persia, Afghanistan and Tibet was signed, together with the appendix to it (on the Chumbi Valley) and exchange letters (notes on scientific expeditions).

While realizing that the convention was a link in the chain of British moves towards Tibet, the Russian diplomats missed their opportunity to prevent this chain from being further strengthened.

Minister of Foreign Affairs Izvolskiy noted that "as a real equivalent to the stable position that England has persistently striven for since 1890 (the year of concluding the Anglo-Chinese Convention on Tibet and Sikkim - N.K.) and which she has finally achieved through a number of international agreements, we can counterpoise only the needs of our Buddhists and the scientific achievements of our Russian explorers of Tibet. "The London cabinet, certainly fully aware of its advantage in status, has displayed an indubitable readiness to repudiate its exclusive claims, but we cannot consider this circumstance alone to be sufficiently satisfactory for us. But then, if the Tibetan affair is regarded as a touchstone for determining the sincerity of the mutual Anglo-Russian intention to reach a general accord, our answer must exclude any petty cavils at immaterial details, which may cause only distrust on the part of England and difficulties to the affairs of paramount state importance on schedule now."[13]

The advantages that Britain enjoyed were not limited to those pointed out by Izvolskiy. Her main advantage was an opportunity to play first violin in deciding the fate of Tibet. Being master of the situation and full of initiative in this field, she could make things appear as if she were displaying "a broad view on the subject", disdaining "immaterial details", and so on. But while setting the fashion, in reality she was also compelling her partners, in this case Russia, to play into her hand. This detail escaped the attention of the Russian diplomatic corps; or, at least, Izvolskiy, having overlooked it, was heading straight into the outspread net. Palitsyn, a representative of Russian military circles and the recipient of the above-cited Izvolskiy letter, was likewise far from a realistic evaluation of the issue when he wrote in his answer: "...in the case of Tibet, we are, so to speak, free from English pressure."[14] Indeed, the pressure was there, but invisible, and the Russian diplomatic corps was playing up to the British.

As opposed to Izvolskiy, who was inclined to ignore the "needs of our Buddhists and the scientific achievements of our Russian explorers of Tibet", Palitsyn expressed at that time a somewhat different point of view when discussing Tibetan problems: "We do not have any direct frontier or military interests in Tibet. But we do have certain moral interests concerning Tibet formed in the course of our history (implying because of the Buddhists in Russia—N.K.). This moral interest in Tibet may probably be spectral, but nevertheless it does exist and should be taken into consideration."[15]

In the same source, when writing about the absence of British pressure, he noted: "England now finds it desirable to obtain from us both confirmation of what she has already actually firmly established through her agreements with Tibet and China, and at the same time our promise not to communicate directly with the Dalai Lama...And if this concession is necessary, we should make it only in exchange for something real and indeed advantageous for us."

Palitsyn's point of view on transacting with Great Britain over Tibetan issues coincides with Pokotilov's opinion, who also objected to the Russian diplomatic corps' "free-of-charge" renunciation of its positions in exchange for illusory British "concessions". The latter had not been Great Britain's renunciation of her Tibetan plans, but merely a natural development of her Tibetan policy regardless of Russia's position. Following in the fairway of British policy, Palitsyn wrote, "we would reject our moral interests in Tibet in return for such English promises as have already been given to China."[16]

Thus it is evident that Palitsyn had come very close to understanding the role of Tibet in Anglo-Chinese relations. These relations were being built at the expense of Tibet and to the prejudice of Tibet by mutual consent between Britain and China, while the British party was involving Russia in Tibetan affairs only as a certain kind of guarantor confirming the Anglo-Chinese deals with her authority.

When one puts the convention of 1907 into sequence with the other international agreements concluded by Britain at the beginning of the 20th century, one may soundly assert that the primary goal of the British party was to achieve in this case international recognition of Chinese suzerainty over Tibet. On the other hand, the head of the British cabinet maintained that the convention was aimed at reaching an agreement "about the minor states in order to avoid disturbances between the Great Powers".[17]

The necessity to avoid disturbances resulted from the tension mounting on the European continent, where the polarization of forces, outlined by the Anglo-French agreement of 1904, had led in the course of its development to the close Anglo-French-Russian union under the name of the Entente. The convention of 1907 on Persia, Afghanistan and Tibet was removing the last traces of suspicion and "disturbances" between Russia and Britain.

Chapter Eight

The dragon by the gates of India

During the last period of their rule in China, the Manchu Ch'ing dynasty pursued a very active policy in central Asia—in both Mongolia and Tibet—to subdue these two countries to the status they had (in the 18th century) at the time of the Ch'ien-lung emperor. This splash of energy was sometimes difficult for foreign diplomats to understand. Why all the fuss about such distant places, when there were so many really urgent problems unsolved much closer to the capital, which should demand all the attention for years to come?

The process of establishing Ch'ing power in Tibet became possible due to British assistance. But it started to develop so successfully that the Chinese felt they did not need any further support. Therefore, they attempted to undermine or, preferably, completely bring to nil any British prestige in the region, where Britain had shown her military force impressively enough. The situation, however, turned out to be considerably less stable than expected, to the detriment of British interests.

The Russian threat had never become anything more than an un-materialized phantom. As regards the menace to India from the other side, China, the Russian diplomatic representative in Simla wrote that "this time England has come to face no longer an imaginary, but a real—though, probably, still a very remote—threat."[1] According to this line of thinking, the British policy that had caused this threat to appear created the preconditions for its realization too. It took the shape of a border war in the Himalayas half a century later.

British politicians watched Ch'ing ambitions in regions next to India grow and cause unforeseen complications. In an article about the new threat to India, P. Landon expressed his alarm in connection with such development of the situation. According to him, Tibet, instead of being a buffer state, had become a province of China. It was governed with inconceivable cruelty by a proconsul possessing absolute power and an occupation army that stood at the gates of India. The ease of capturing Tibet had inflamed Chinese desire, directing them towards domains that were undoubtedly

Indian. The Maharajah of Nepal was taking the case so seriously that he informed the author of the article about the preparations he was carrying out to annex, if necessary, the southern part of Tibet in order to secure a glacis for his protection. Even Lord Morley took the trouble to assure the government of Bhutan that they could always rely on Indian troops in defence against any Chinese invasion.

Obviously Nepal, true to her traditional policy of surviving as an independent state between two great neighbors—British India and China—was seriously considering the inevitable necessity to stand up for her independence. Sikkim, according to the Anglo-Chinese Convention of 1890, was a British protectorate. Bhutan, the third of the minor Himalayan states at which Chinese fists were being shaken, was under the influence of British India, starting from the second half of the 19th century.

Now, however, the Ch'ing authorities were trying to change things. The amban in Lhasa sent a letter to the Maharajah of Bhutan, informing him of the forthcoming stationing of Chinese troops within the territory of his country. The official title of Maharajah as an independent ruler of state was ignored in the letter, which treated him like a subordinate. The British colonial authorities hurriedly concluded the treaty with Bhutan, providing for closer links between the two parties. Non-interference in domestic affairs was guaranteed to Bhutan, while in her foreign policy she was to consult the government of Britain. Thus the actual British protectorate over Bhutan was made official.

The British authorities would not let Manchu Ch'ing troops pass through Indian territory for fear of the influence on India of a Tibetan liberation movement. But Chinese officials used this route freely. At the end of 1906, Chang Yin-t'ang, the new Ch'ing representative in Tibet, went to Lhasa through India without hindrance. Soon the British saw that he was re-organizing the system of Chinese government in Tibet and, while doing so, was destroying any remnants of British prestige and influence to the north of the Himalayan ridge.

Chang Yin-t'ang had achieved a marked success in this respect. Nothing could have helped him better than the British renunciation of the most effective aspects of Curzon's policy in Tibet and, later, her negotiations with China (on the convention of 1906) and with Russia in St Petersburg. Representatives of the Indian colonial administration and Ch'ing emissaries demonstrated mutual dislike when coming into business contact on Tibetan territory. The colonialist views of British officers fostered by their prolonged ruling sway in India, with their estranged attitude towards the native population, clashed with the traditional presumption of Ch'ing officials in their relations with foreigners.

The following notable episode, which took place during Chang Yin-t'ang's journey through India to Lhasa at the beginning of 1906, may serve as a vivid example. During his stay in a Chinese yamen in the Chumbi Valley, Chang Yin-t'ang had completely ignored Lieutenant Campbell. The latter was a representative of British India, which occupied the valley according to the convention of 1904. Campbell had been sure that the Chinese official would pay a visit to him, the ruler of the valley. But he waited in vain. And when he had tried to show who was master and had set out for the yamen himself in full dress, he was told by Chang Yin-t'ang's servants to enter through the back door for subordinates. Campbell refused to do so, at which point the servants told him that Chang Yin-t'ang was out.

This episode was not an exception, and this was well known to anyone who had come in contact with Ch'ing officials. Their traditional way of behavior was characterized in a message by the Russian consulate in India: "Just like his chief (Tang Shao-yi), Chang Yin-t'ang belongs to those Chinese who were educated in America, speak English and think much of themselves. In all their contacts with foreigners, these gentry adhere to an obstructionist tactic intended to show their countrymen that their foreign education had not in the least made them compliant to "overseas barbarians". On the contrary, it had armed them with "a reliable weapon for successive struggle with the latter's solicitations"."[2]

Nevertheless, these unfriendly relations between Chinese and Indo-British officials in Tibet did not prevent the governments of both parties from pursuing a mutually beneficial policy. In April, 1909 the Russian diplomatic mission in India pointed out in a report based on materials from the local press that "recently China has managed to restore her suzerainty over Tibet owing to the complete neglect of benefits, legally gained due to Younghusband's expedition, on the part of the English."[3]

The Russian diplomatic mission in Peking also noted that after the Anglo-Chinese agreement on Tibet had been concluded, "the Peking government started unflinchingly to seek the gradual destruction of the vast independence of the Dalai Lama and Tibetan clergy exercised in domestic government issues, the independence for which had existed up to that time...For the time being, the government of China has found it necessary to act extremely warily with respect to Tibet. But this will be only up to the moment when the status of China in regions next to Tibet will have become strong enough to let her carry out large-scale political and economical reforms in this country openly...Last autumn (in 1909), it was decided to send the first echelon of Chinese troops to Tibet immediately—a detachment consisting of 5,000 soldiers under the command of Colonel Chung Ying...The most serious obstacles are the extreme remoteness of Tibet from the centre and the complete lack of ways of communication. These difficulties have prevented the detachment from reaching its destination."[4]

The restoration of Chinese-Manchu "influence" in Tibet was actually a military conquest. By the end of 1909, Ch'ing troops had invaded the Tibetan regions of Batang, Derge and Chamdo. Lhasa was still far away. After Younghusband's mission, the prestige of Ch'ing authority could be established only by force of arms. Both Chang Yin-t'ang and the amban in Lhasa, Lien Yu, and his officials did not have enough armed forces at their disposal for solving this task. Their wish to consolidate their power and set up a new order could be realized only to a small extent because of the general opposition of the Tibetans, which threatened to grow into an open, armed anti-Manchu struggle.

By that time, the army of General Chao Erh-feng was meant to help the Chinese officials in Lhasa. But, being stationed in the eastern outlying districts of Tibet, it was separated from Lhasa by a vast, almost impassable country populated by inhabitants who were disposed to be hostile. The population of these outlying districts were semi-independent Tibetan tribes who did not obey the Dalai Lama and were not included in the administrative system of the Ch'ing empire. Attempts had already been made in 1903 to subordinate them to Manchu power. But it was Chao Erh-feng who really took them in hand, starting from 1906. At that time, he was appointed "supreme commissioner for frontier affairs" (Pien-wu Ta-ch'en). In 1907, he started to introduce the administrative system of districts to these territories, with the centre in Batang. This military-administrative organizational activity was drawn out until 1911, due to resistance by the local population.

Chao Erh-feng implemented cruel measures to achieve his objective. This "liberator from the monastic yoke", as he called himself in his appeals to local inhabitants, mercilessly executed and put to death both monks and farmers, and burned down innumerable Buddhist sanctuaries and dwellings. His soldiers defiled Buddhist holy objects, destroyed sacred books and melted down Buddha statues for copper coins and bullets. Not having acquired a reputation as an administrative figure, he became known to Tibetans as "executioner Chao".

However, following the example of Sir J. Jordan, a British envoy in Peking, the literature has characterized Chao Erh-feng and his brother Chao Erh-hsün, who was governor general of Szechuan, as able administrators. According to emperor's edict, these two figures were to bring Tibet to obedience through their joint efforts. Jordan wrote that Chao Erh-hsün had the reputation of being the most steadfast and able official of the empire...This 68-year-old little man with a wrinkled face was proud of the fact that he had never smoked in his life and had drunk no more than tea, and that the three years of his office as governor general of Szechuan were enough for him to wipe out all cultivation of the opium poppy there. The Chinese policy with respect to Tibet at the time was, according to Jordan, mostly the handiwork of Chao Erh-hsün and Chao Erh-feng.

According to the *Ch'ing-shih Kao* (Chronicle of Ch'ing History), the Ch'ing Court had received numerous proposals concerning their policy in Tibet. But the Chinese documents state that there were no other means at the disposal of the government to make the Tibetans obey except military might, although they had intended to adopt these other proposals.

In the autumn of 1909, Chao Erh-feng's troops seized Chamdo, the last town in the so-called frontier eastern Tibet regions that separated Chao Erh-feng from Tibet itself. Now he was on the verge of seizing Lhasa and thus accomplishing his main task—to establish Ch'ing power in the country. A mobile unit was formed consisting of 2,000 soldiers, with General Chung Ying at its head. Shortly afterwards, Chung Ying was to play a notable role in Tibetan affairs, when the curtain was dropping and the last attempts of the Ch'ing authorities to establish their supremacy in Tibet were falling to the ground.

The entry of Chung Ying's detachment on to the territory of Tibet itself marked a new stage in the direct military capture of the country. In Lhasa, the amban Lien Yu was using all his diplomatic abilities to try to persuade the local Tibetan authorities not to put up resistance to Chung Ying because, he pretended, the latter was marching to Central Tibet in order to perform police duties at trade markets. These functions, in accordance with the conventions of 1904 and 1906, were previously fulfilled by Anglo-Indian troops. But by this time, they had left the country, as had been specified by the trade regulations of 1908.

The Tibetan Kashag cabinet, in objection to this, suggested that markets could be guarded by their own police, if it became necessary, These objections were accompanied by demands to withdraw Chinese troops from Tibetan territory. But these protests and demands did not impress the amban. He, together with his assistant, continued to assure the Tibetan authorities that Chung Ying posed no danger to them.

At an audience with the Dalai Lama that was also attended by the Nepalese representative, the assistant amban stressed again that the Ch'ing armed forces were intended only to guard markets. On arrival in Lhasa, they would be distributed among the markets and not interfere in the home affairs of Tibet. He even promised to give proper written guarantees.

Indeed, written guarantees came from him the next day. But, instead of non-interference in home affairs, they contained a statement about non-interference in the religious affairs of the Dalai Lama, which were, as it was, objectively out of Chinese control. This was a blunt fraud. As the official Chinese chronicle *Ch'ing-shih Kao* informs us, Chung Ying's detachment, recruited from the Szechuan army, was to remain at the command and under the control of the amban in Tibet.

The far-fetchedness of this pretence for bringing troops into Tibet was obvious to an outside observer even in those times. The newspaper *Sankt-Peterburgskie Vedomosti* wrote: "After the extremely deplorable latest events in Tibet, when the Chinese, who based their Great Power policy in Asia on the external honoring of an archaic strange cult, had decided, in this case, to treat the spiritual ruler of the Lamaist world sternly...The invasion of the English there in 1904 gave the Peking government cause and example for stretching their hand more imperiously towards the holy city of the Dalai Lama."[5]

The amban in Lhasa and his assistant kept on spouting mellifluous speeches. They scarcely could set the Tibetans completely at ease and lull their vigilance. Still, they succeeded in achieving their main goal—Lhasa did not send out a covering detachment to meet Chung Ying. And when the Lhasa authorities saw that Chung Ying's detachment was twice as large as the amban had told them, and that his intentions had nothing to do with police service, it was already too late to organize any resistance.

Chung Ying's soldiers reached Lhasa on February 12, 1910. They were met by the amban's guard on the banks of the Kyi-chu River. When marching into the city, they started firing their guns at Tibetan policemen, many of whom were killed or injured. They also met a gross of lamas on their way to a Lhasa temple, headed by one of the most respected Tibetan ecclesiastics. The Chinese soldiers beat them mercilessly, tore off their robes and then killed almost all of them.[6] They even opened fire on the Potala as well.

From the very beginning of their stay in Lhasa, Chung Ying's soldiers behaved like thugs, committing violence, robberies and motiveless murders. This lasted for nearly two years, up to the time of the Xin-hai Revolution of 1911, which became a significant landmark in the history of relations between the two countries.

As soon as Chung Ying's detachment had reached Lhasa, Chao Erh-feng moved his troops to Za-yul district situated to the north of Assam, near the Indian border. The English newspaper *Morning Post* wrote on February 10, 1910: "A great empire, the future military strength of which no man can foresee, has suddenly appeared on the northeast frontier of India. The problem of the northwest frontier thus bids fair to be duplicated in the long run, and a double pressure placed on the defensive resources of the Indian empire"...China, in a word, has come to the gates of India.[7]

Nowadays, this newspaper passage has become a widespread citation. It seems to be predicting the beginning of a new stage in Sino-Indian relations—the stage we observe at present, when these relations are complicated by border territorial disagreements that grow to the extent of open conflict. It has resulted in a military clash between the two countries in the Himalayan War of 1962.

This newspaper passage has been quoted by the authors of the most significant works on the Sino-Indian border—by A. Lamb, D. Woodman, N. Maxwell and others. In all these cases the question discussed was the strategic threat to Assam. Establishing Chinese control over the whole of Tibet inevitably meant to them control over the southern and southwestern regions, as well as over the fertile Indian valleys beyond.

As previously explained, the Sino-Indian border and territorial controversy that flared up in the mid-50s, resulting in the 1962 Himalayan War, has caused the active development of the theme of our narration. It was quite natural to look to the past for the roots of this conflict. History was to give answers to questions concerning the present, hence a heightened interest in Himalayan processes at the beginning of the century, as that was the time when this region attracted attention, for the first time, as an arena of international policy.

It was also natural that Chao Erh-feng's military actions in the Tibetan districts next to India produced the impression of their being a rehearsal for the Himalayan War of 1962 and for the capture of territories to the south of the main Himalayan ridge. This line of reasoning is meant, then, precisely to prove the continuity of aggressive Chinese policy from 1909 to 1962, thus forming a bridge linking the past and the present.

One would think that a logical and simple explanation of the past like this would give a key to understanding the present. But we must acknowledge that this would be too simple to be true. It is quite evident that such an extrapolation is wrong. First of all, it would be a mistake to regard Anglo-Chinese relations with respect to Tibet at that time as the relations between hostile parties. There is no doubt that the "Russian threat" to Tibet gave England an opportunity to suppress Tibet in 1904. It also helped Ch'ing authorities establish their supremacy there by means of the Lhasa and the Peking Conventions, although this final objective was never attained in the end. But later, after the Entente had been formed, the notorious Russian threat could not serve as an excuse for developing the Anglo-Chinese alliance on Tibet any longer. Nevertheless, former British policy concerning Tibet and China remained without change. The Ch'ing position stayed the same as well. Both parties, Ch'ing China and imperialist Britain, continued in accord to pursue the identical policy of suppressing liberation movements and aspirations for independence in the region.

Those were groundless fears, then, that the *Morning Star* provoked in its readers, intimidating them with the report that "China has come up to the gates of India", as before they had intimidated them with a Russian threat to India. Both the Russian and Chinese threats to India were a product of imagination brought to life by misgivings about the stability of the system ruling the sub-continent. But the true threat to this system lay in the factors, not external but internal, that ruined it 40 years later.

Chinese aggressiveness on the northeastern frontiers of India and the accumulation of strength there were, in the opinion of the local colonial officers, a challenge to British supremacy, at least in the tribal territories. But from the heights of the London government, which did not share their anxiety, it did not look so formidable.

The Ch'ing "clenching of fists" over the minor Himalayan states did not bring any practical results. However panicking or sensational were reports about Chao Erh-feng's troops emerging on the Indian borders, no consequences followed. In the end, the outlined threat to the British estates dematerialized completely. The British colonial authorities' attention in the direction of the Tibetan borders decreased to the point of indifference. Interests in Tibet, in their own turn, were focused on resisting Chao Erh-feng's troops. In this respect, the Tibetans were acting at their own peril and could not hope to receive any help from anywhere.

CHAPTER NINE

The heavenly Tsar and the worldly Tsar

The wanderings of the Dalai Lama after his flight from Lhasa deserve special attention. The Ch'ing emperor's edict of August 28, 1904, about the Dalai Lama's "dismissal" from his post did not have any practical results. In less than two years, the Russian envoy to China, Pokotilov, received a savory offer, which looked more like a provocation based on the well-known sympathetic attitude of the Russians towards the Dalai Lama. On May 8, 1906 he reported to St Petersburg: "A person close to the court circles declared to me that he is capable of carrying out a promulgation by the Chinese government of an act that would be desirable to the Dalai Lama, namely restoring the latter's prestige in Tibet; but he demanded that for this he should be given a bribe of 30,000 roubles. I replied evasively."[1] No answer was received to this offer from St Petersburg.

Not only the Ch'ing authorities, but the British imperialists were also making efforts to get rid of the obstinate Dalai Lama. By the end of 1905, the Panchen Lama had come to India, and the British were going to use him for their own purposes. Klemm reported from Bombay that Tibetans, headed by the Panchen Lama, were sent to Rawalpandi "in time for the conclusion of major manoeuvres, so that they should be present at a large military parade. Local newspapers are eulogizing this wise decision of the government and saying that contemplating an army of almost 60,000 soldiers at the above-mentioned parade has produced a stunning, and thus very useful, impression on the Tibetans."[2]

Beside psychologically impressing the Panchen Lama by demonstrating to him British military force and intimidating him, the colonial government had tried to influence him in other ways as well. In a letter of the Panchen Lama to the Dalai Lama, it was said that "the English presented him with a gift of 50,000 langs of silver and proposed him to become a candidate to the throne of Tibet instead of the Dalai Lama. The money was readily taken by the Panchen Lama, but he absolutely rejected the candidature...."[3]

Meanwhile, in January of 1905, a delegation arrived in Urga from Tibet inviting the Dalai Lama to return to Lhasa. So long as

Peking and London had a negative attitude towards such a return, the newly arrived Tibetans together with the Dalai Lama came to the conclusion that a return would inevitably lead to the necessity of co-operating with the British and, consequently, to acknowledging that the resistance offered against them had been illegal. On the other hand, the Ch'ing authorities apprehended that "the high priest, with his influence, would prevent them from consolidating their position in Lhasa, which apparently is the main goal of Chinese policy with respect to Tibet at the present moment," the Russian envoy to Peking wrote. "I considered it my duty to exchange thoughts with Chinese ministers about the desirability of promulgating some governmental act directed at restoring the high priest's prestige in Tibet. The Chinese replied, however, elusively."[4]

The Russian envoy did not subsequently abandon these kind of attempts. He informed his superiors about one of his talks with the Wai-wu Pu (the Chinese ministry of foreign affairs): "During an explanation concerning the Dalai Lama, I met with a great discretion and evasiveness exceeding the usual on the part of the Wai-wu Pu. Prince Ch'ing echoed ignorance about the Dalai Lama's decision to go to Lhasa. I managed to obtain only rather uncertain assertions that the Chinese government did not mean to hinder the Dalai Lama in his choice of route he would use to arrive in Tibet. But, at the same time, Prince Ch'ing said that the mode of action taken by the Chinese government with respect to the Dalai Lama would depend on a decision made by the Empress Dowager."[5]

The blank wall of ill-will erected by the Ch'ing government remained impenetrable, and the envoy did no more than conceal his impatience when he reported: "The Chinese are answering with wittingly mendacious assurances that everything is being done in accordance with the Dalai Lama's wishes."[6]

An intention appeared within the circles around the Dalai Lama to seek the assistance of France and Germany in returning him to Lhasa. Khitrovo, the head of the Russian expedition to Mongolia, in a detailed message of July, 1906, based on Mongolian sources, mentioned that "some parties of Tibetans say that, in view of Russian elusion, it is necessary to choose another state, possibly one friendly to Russia. But the Dalai Lama has persistently stood his ground to rely, for the time being, exclusively on Russia. In the Dalai Lama's opinion, support and patronage on the part of Russia should manifest themselves in acknowledging the fair character of the Tibetan and Mongolian lawful demands,[7] accepting the Dalai

Lama's representations on the matter and bringing them up for discussion and decision by all the great European powers which, the Dalai Lama is sure, cannot but agree with the fairness of these demands."[8]

It is impossible to overestimate Khitrovo's role in Tibetan issues. His long stay in Mongolia gave him an opportunity to obtain a profound knowledge of relations between Mongolia and Tibet. The Russian command was aware that the Dalai Lama was acquainted with Khitrovo, and "had sent him presents, which caused him to write return letters that had a purely polite character and in no way dealt with political issues." Later, in February, 1906 the Army Group Commander in the Far East ordered that "contacts between Lieutenant-Colonel Khitrovo and the Tibetan high priest be interrupted." When informing the minister of foreign affairs on this matter, the Chief of General Staff explained that Khitrovo had sent "absolutely privately, without any official orders, his officer Kostritskiy" on a mission, whom the Dalai Lama had expressed his wish to see. "During this meeting, Kostritskiy did not tell the Dalai Lama anything on behalf of the Russian authorities, but simply listened to what the Dalai Lama had to say, which he reported to his chief."[9]

During the Dalai Lama's stay in Peking, Dorjiev was also present, having arrived from St Petersburg. This circumstance was the focus of attention of the diplomatic corps in Peking. Representatives of the Great Powers understood all the significance of what was happening before their eyes. Only the Russian embassy avoided any contacts with the Tibetans.

In the autumn of 1908, State Counsellor Korostovets communicated to St Petersburg: "Dorjiev asks me when I contemplate visiting the Dalai Lama, who reportedly expressed his amazement that the Russian representative had not been to him yet, while envoys from France and the United States had paid their visits. I explained that I am going to visit the high priest in the nearest future, and that superfluous haste could arouse the suspicion of China and England. The Dalai Lama apparently considered envoys' visits to be desirable for raising his prestige in the eyes of the Chinese and as a recognition of an independent status."[10]

The Russian envoy to Peking, invested with the great confidence of St Petersburg and recommended to the Dalai Lama as such, was aware of "the intentions among the Dalai Lama's retainers to seek help in other places" and did not see any need to make obstacles for those who would carry out such a search. "In view of our friendship with these states," he wrote, "if the Dalai Lama really wished to return to Tibet, addressing them could only prove useful. The success of such an alliance will save us the trouble of a rather complicated and difficult rendering of our hospitality to the Dalai Lama in Russia, which could be necessary in the extreme case."[11]

The attitude of the Russian envoy to the Tibetans' intentions to address other foreign states had its explanation in the invariable position of the Russian government as a whole. He saw that "the Dalai Lama now is seriously thinking about an open rupture with China, hoping to move to Russia. In the instructions given to me on my appointment to Peking, it was stated quite definitely that the Russian government regards the Buddhist high priest's return to Tibet as the best way to solve this problem and I was supposed to act on this pretext during my forthcoming meeting with the Dalai Lama, as well as in my future contacts with the Chinese government.

"At present, the Dalai Lama considers his return to Tibet to be possible only on condition of receiving our rather positive assurances as regards our active protection of Tibet against aggressive plans on the part of England. Admitting the desirability of the Dalai Lama's returning to Tibet as soon as possible, we must, as one would think, avoid arousing separatist thoughts with respect to China on the part of the Buddhist high priest. We must try to convince him, little by little, to return to Tibet, because in the case of his absence from this country being too long, he is undoubtedly running the risk of losing a considerable share of his political influence, which is his only possible effective weapon in the forthcoming strife of Tibet against the aggressive plans of England."[12]

There is no need to comment on Pokotilov's report. It reaffirmed once more the Tibetan policy of Russia, and her benevolent attitude towards the Dalai Lama as an influential figure in the eyes of the Tibetans and all Buddhists, including those who were Russian. And this made his return to Tibet indispensable in order to avoid loss of influence there. At the same time, the Tibetan policy of Russia was neighborly to China. Specifically, she appraised with a great deal of restraint the "separatist thoughts with respect to China on the part of the Buddhist high priest", although she had to take into consideration that these thoughts were, to a considerable extent, stimulated by Curzon's aggressive policy and its unambiguous support by the Ch'ing authorities.

However, the plans to address other foreign states were not realized despite the positive attitude of Russia, with whose representatives the Dalai Lama had consulted. Neither France nor Germany were interested in defending Tibetan independence or in strife against encroachments upon it. For a year, these plans were revived from time to time, but finally they were rejected. In an official note to the imperial name it was reported: "As for the thought expressed by the Dalai Lama about addressing foreign states for the purpose of establishing joint patronage over Tibet, this proposal, seemingly, does not deserve attention as having any practical grounds and thus should be rejected, as well as the project of now sending a Russian expedition to Tibet."[13] The above-mentioned project of sending a Russian expedition to Tibet originated from the Tibetan side.

At the beginning of 1906, Dorjiev, who continued to perform the foreign policy missions of the Dalai Lama, wrote to the Russian minister of foreign affairs that "His Holiness the Dalai Lama desired to point out to me that I should, upon a preliminary agreement with the Russian government, address the other Great Powers in order to establish friendly relations with them and achieve their joint patronage over Tibet."[14] But so long as this task remained unaccomplished, Dorjiev tried at least to guarantee the personal safety of the Dalai Lama.

In his letter to the minister, Dorjiev "obediently requested to be granted a letter of assurance to be dispatched to His Holiness the Dalai Lama, and copies of pledges of the Chinese as well as the English governments, concerning the inviolability of the Dalai Lama's person and his prestige in Tibet...For my part, considering the Dalai Lama's return to Lhasa to be desirable, I cannot at the same time pass over in silence the question of sending an expedition to Lhasa on the part of Russian government (at least, incognito). This expedition could become a witness of possible acts of violence in Tibet."

Dorjiev backed his request for sending an expedition by alluding to "the best and influential persons in Tibet, who fully sympathise with it." Dorjiev's fears were caused by information he had received that "the attitude of the Chinese government towards the Dalai Lama is becoming abusive. To all appearances, one may expect violent measures."[15]

This expedition was also to perform scientific functions, in which respect Dorjiev pointed out that "the urgent need for sending Russian expeditions (to Tibet) is evident. Their aim is to gather collections and information on both natural history and ethnography. Gathering information and collections on ethnography is time-consuming, and that is why the expedition should last a long time. In view of this, it is desirable that in connection with an expedition to Central Tibet, a permanent station should be organized in a mountainous region of Tibet, to last for the entire period of the expedition, where meteorological observations important for exploring Tibetan climatic conditions might also be carried out. It is desirable that the expedition should set out already in the spring (of 1906)."[16] Thus Dorjiev was trying to use the scientific interest of Russian orientalists in Tibet for political purposes as well.

Plans to encourage the Russian government's interest in the religious circles around the Dalai Lama were also being worked out. This could be achieved by convoking a Buddhist ecumenical council for solving various religious questions. Pokotilov, however, wrote about it: "I dare think that the very fact of convoking such a council is scarcely of particular importance for the Dalai Lama. He and his counsellors are undoubtedly interested only in provoking—even if artificially—some act, in the development of which our government should have to operate jointly with the Buddhist high priest, and this to prove in public a certain community of common interests. I put this project on the same level with the high priest's solicitations to make official the affair of sending a Russian escort on a mission with him, of appointing an official Russian agent (representative) to Lhasa, of expressing on our part guarantees for his personal safety, and so on. In view of the extreme persistence of the Dalai Lama and his counsellors in this direction, I have taken the liberty to propose to you a measure that could satisfy the high priest, while being entirely inoffensive at the same time. That is to thank the Dalai Lama officially, on imperial behalf, for his beneficial influence on Buddhist pilgrims who have thronged from Trans-Baikalya to see him."[17]

Of course, the "measure" proposed by Pokotilov did not in the least meet the expectations of the Tibetan exiles. Nevertheless, they did not abandon their plans to involve the Russian party with Tibetan affairs, as well as to procure guarantees for the Dalai Lama's personal safety. Official restraint on the Russian part was being displayed against a background of streams of Buryat pilgrims from

Trans-Baikalya gathering in Urga in huge numbers. When it became known that the Dalai Lama intended to set forth on his way back to Tibet, "some of his most devoted followers", according to Dorjiev's information, "expressed their resolve to accompany the high priest all the way to his place of permanent residence in order to serve as his guard."[18]

The persistence of the Tibetans in securing his safety had its own reasons. The attitude of Ch'ing government functionaries towards the Dalai Lama was not becoming any less hostile over the course of time. The most influential Ch'ing dignitary, "the strongest person except for the Empress Dowager", Prince Ch'ing, had demanded from the Tibetans a bribe of 260,000 langs of silver for "an intercession in Tibetan affairs for settling issues with the English and with his own government."

The Tibetans, however, refused to give the bribe, considering that "the expense would be an entirely aimless waste, because it is impossible to rely upon any support or help, either on the part of Prince Ch'ing, or from any other Chinese dignitaries. And most convincing in this respect is the Chinese attitude the Dalai Lama has experienced in Tibet and later on his arrival in Mongolia."[19]

Ambans, sent to Mongolia from Peking to negotiate with the Dalai Lama, behaved arrogantly and overbearingly. A Russian consular official, Kuzminskiy, stressed the hostility of the Chinese towards the high priest. At the same time, in his memorandum on his visit to the Dalai Lama in July, 1906, Kuzminskiy reported that he had brought to the Dalai Lama's notice "the guarantees of inviolability, that seemed weighty enough, repeatedly expressed by Prince Ch'ing in talks with our envoys."[20]

The British threat was no less than that of the Ch'ing. This was a matter of particular concern for the Russian ministry of foreign affairs. Figures well known in connection with Tibetan problems such as P. P. Semionov, A. P. Ignatev, F. F. Palitsyn, S. F. Oldenburg, E. E. Ukhtomskiy, P. K. Kozlov and others, took part in the conference, where the minister of foreign affairs pointed out the reasons for such concern: "We have information about an extremely hostile attitude towards the possible arrival of the Dalai Lama at his former residence on the part of the English, who, apparently, are ready to undertake extreme measures. It goes without saying that any misfortune that might befall the Dalai Lama, who is supposed to be going to Lhasa with a Russian escort—under the Russian flag, so to speak—would cause serious harm to our prestige."[21]

From the moment of the high priest's arrival in Urga, the Dalai Lama's safety and concern for his "future settlement" were always in the sight of the Russian foreign ministry. In this connection, a suggestion was made to take the opportunity of using the services of the Russian traveller, P. K. Kozlov, who was also in Urga at that time. It was proposed that he, with his escort, accompany the Dalai Lama to the borders of Tibet.

The ministry realized, however, that sending a Russian detachment through Chinese territory could give rise to some "misunderstanding or censure on the part of the government of China", so the Russian envoy to Peking was authorized to discuss the matter with Chinese ministers. As a result of bilateral consultations, "the consul in Urga has been instructed to tell the Dalai Lama that, in view of the categorical guarantees of his safety during the journey expressed by the Chinese government, the government of Russia does not consider it possible to send Captain Kozlov on the mission. The letter concerning this matter, which was delivered to our envoy by Prince Ch'ing, gives us the right to make the Chinese government fully responsible for the slightest misfortune that might occur on the way."[22]

Kozlov's appearance in Mongolia and his meetings with the Dalai Lama were not the result of some Russian government plan. The minister of war, in March, 1905, wrote about it to the foreign minister: "The chairman of the Russian Geographic Society has informed me that the Tibetan expedition of 1899-1901, headed by Captain Kozlov, to a considerable extent owed its success to the patronage and benevolence towards Russian travellers to Tibet on the part of the Dalai Lama himself. Presently, the Geographic Society, profiting from the occasion of the Dalai Lama's stay in Urga, regards it as its moral duty to express in some way its sincere appreciation to the ruler of Tibet for such a friendly attitude towards representatives of Russia, and solicits for Captain Kozlov to be sent on a mission to Urga in order to greet the Dalai Lama."[23]

Kozlov had given the Dalai Lama regards on behalf of the Russian Geographic Society during a meeting with him. As for his further scientific expeditions to Tibet, according to a record of the talk, "the Dalai Lama asked to communicate that there would be no obstacles on the part of the government of Tibet for an open journey of Russians to Tibet for scientific and commercial purposes. On the contrary, they would be met with accustomed hospitality and assistance. For all matters concerning Tibet, Tsannyit Khambo

Agvan Dorjiev will be left in Russia as charge d'affaires, and the Dalai Lama asks to render him favor with appropriate confidence and attention. The Dalai Lama also asks for permission to avail himself of 25 Buryat-Cossacks (for his return to Lhasa) with a disciplined senior Cossack combat sergeant at their head. The cost of maintaining this detachment would be paid by the Dalai Lama out of his own funds, but he asks to accept the time of their service in Tibet as active duty."[24]

Kozlov's expedition itself included only a few persons: N. Ya. Kozhevnikov, a portrait painter and instructor at Real school in Troitsesavsk; P. Teleshov, a technical scout and Cossack sergeant of the Trans-Baikalyan Cossack troops; G. Badmazhapov, a collector of insects; and Ya Afushin, an interpreter. In March 1907, Kozlov sent a note to the Russian foreign ministry and general headquarters requesting permission for one more trip, which read: "As a geographer, ethnographer and naturalist, I am most allured by a journey to that place. Carrying on with the mission I once took upon myself—exploring central Asia—I regard it as my moral duty, not to mention my passionate desire, to set off to that same place once again and to work there with all my energy and ability for the sake of the sciences of geography and natural history".[25]

The military administration, to which Kozlov was directly subordinate, did not object to such a trip. General headquarters commander F. Palitsyn wrote to Foreign Minister Lamsdorff: "This expedition, organized by the Geographic Society at its own expense, with political or military purposes being totally alien to it, has, as its exclusive task, the scientific investigation of hitherto poorly explored regions...Taking into consideration all the above-stated, and with deep sympathy for the task of the expedition, I have the honor to ask Your Excellency not to refuse to inform me of your resolution."[26]

The government of Russia did not establish official relations with the Dalai Lama. They apprehended that "an appointment of a Russian functionary could have the most serious consequences for him on the part of the Peking government".[27] They could not even render the Dalai Lama financial assistance, considering that "granting him a subsidy, which would be impossible to conceal from the Chinese, could only do him harm, not to mention that it would be difficult to forward such subsidy to him, and it would probably be used by some outside persons."[28]

At the same time, they were attempting to promote a happy

termination of friction between the Dalai Lama and the Chinese government. The Russian embassy in Peking reported to St Petersburg that, in reply to its request "to permit the Dalai Lama to stay in Urga for some time to receive our Buryat pilgrims,"[29] Chinese ministers answered with the same assertions that the government of China did not put restraint on his freedom and that he might stay in Urga or go to Tibet at his own pleasure.

It is clear, however, from a telegram sent by Lyuba, the Russian consul in Urga, that "these assertions were mendacious, and that the ambans Yang Chih and P'u Shou were demanding in Urga the most quick departure of the Dalai Lama. Any insistence in the face of the Wai-wu Pu would be to no avail and could lead only to his forced dispatch and probable incarceration in some monastery in Inner China. The matter becomes still more complicated due to the fact that messengers from 10 Mongolian princes have visited Peking with the mission of asking for the Dalai Lama's return to Tibet. Of course, this embassy had been initiated by the Khutughtu (Bogdo Khan), whose incomes decreased with the Dalai Lama's arrival. The messengers brought presents for Prince Ch'ing, and so the Chinese government will undoubtedly be considerate towards their application."[30]

But, in fact, the ambans in Urga, Yang Chih and P'u Shou, started to act persistently and unceremoniously. A report was received from the Russian consulate in Urga that the two ambans "came to the Dalai Lama's residence without any warning and demanded a meeting with him. The Dalai Lama, despite ill health, received them. Throughout the entire audience, the ambans behaved proudly and haughtily with respect to the Dalai Lama, and P'u Shou even provocatively. The ambans did their best to make the Dalai Lama leave Urga. Having been questioned about his departure, he answered in the negative, pleading illness and an absence of an answer from Peking to his numerous addresses to the Ch'ing government."[31]

The Dalai Lama, in turn, demanded an answer as to what reasons made the ambans regard his stay in Urga with such hostility. The ambans alleged that it was difficult for the local population to maintain him with his numerous retainers, although it was well known that immediately on arrival in Urga, the Dalai Lama had declared his refusal of any material help.

The talk was far from friendly and, according to a report of a consular official, "The Dalai Lama, sharply interrupting the conversation, said in an excited voice: "In my 12 years of ruling Tibet, I have made a close enough study of you Manchus. I know you well, and I will not let you mock me any longer."[32]

Special messengers came from Peking at last. At a meeting with them, the Dalai Lama "sincerely expressed his opinion about the present regrettable status of Tibet, caused rather by a policy of Chinese ambans in Lhasa and by an indifferent attitude of Peking than by actions of the government of England." Pokotilov, in his message about the dispatch of messengers from Peking, noted that "in Peking they have decided to improve, as far as possible, the attitude towards the Dalai Lama and make him forget old misunderstandings. At any rate, the very fact of the arrival of a Chinese embassy with a letter from the Chinese emperor has a great significance for the high priest."[33]

The words about "old misunderstandings" had been taken by Pokotilov from the letter mentioned above, of which the Dalai Lama did not make a secret. This letter also read: "...from the moment misunderstandings in Tibet began, the Dalai Lama has experienced not a few truly difficult days; and so it is perhaps not without reason that he has expressed displeasure with our government."[34]

The Ch'ing government's compelled, but very limited, acknowledgment of guilt did not, however, promise the Dalai Lama any guarantees of a happy settlement of the situation. He continued his attempts to find a way out in other directions. Since the Russian consulate in Urga was expressing an "amiable, but extremely restrained attitude", the Dalai Lama and his retainers were inclined to think that "the consul in Urga finds contacts to be burdensome and is avoiding meetings with the high priest and his confidants in every way...Having interrupted contacts with the consulate, he (the Dalai Lama) chose to communicate with St Petersburg through the Russian functionary, Mr. Bimbaev, a Buryat whose role was that of a totally private individual."[35]

But, in the end, this way also proved to be of little effect. And as for the Ch'ing messengers, the consul Lyuba wrote to the envoy Pokotilov that "their mutual relations (with the Dalai Lama) threatened to end with a complete break-off. The Dalai Lama's retainers themselves decided to ask the high priest not to annoy the envoys of the Chinese emperor, pleading, among other reasons, the advice repeatedly conveyed by the Russian government to maintain as correct relations with the Chinese as possible...From the very first meeting, the Dalai Lama started to insist on his acquaintance with the complete text of the treaty (the Anglo-Chinese Convention of 1906). At first, the Ch'ing messengers agreed to satisfy his demands, but during subsequent meetings they declared to the Dalai Lama that they had not been authorized to do so."[36]

News about conclusion of the Anglo-Chinese agreement stopped preparations for the Dalai Lama's departure from Urga, which were, as it was, being carried out very unhurriedly even before that. According to a report by the consul Lyuba, the Dalai Lama, "animated by memories of Chinese intrigue and English insidiousness he had had to strive with over the course of the last few years, defended, with heat and conviction, his view on an outward, purely nominal dependence of his country on China. With bitterness, he spoke that China had less than passively reacted to the English infringement of the inviolability of Tibetan territory; that the government of China had remained completely indifferent to his fate after his exile from Tibet; that this time again the Chinese had not bothered to inform him about their conclusion of the treaty with England—of a treaty sealing the fate of Tibet...And presently, the Dalai Lama reports that international relations and circumstances have not altered so much in favor of China that she could assume the rights, belonging exclusively to him, the Dalai Lama, regarding the matter of Tibet's destiny. Basing himself on this proposition, the high priest does not recognize also this treaty, as in its time he did not recognize the convention of the 90th year[37]. He does not recognize it as having for him, the ruler of Tibet, any juridical validity."[38]

The convention of 1906 had been concluded in a way similar to that of the convention of 1890—that is to say, without knowledge or consent of the Tibetans. The deal made at the expense of Tibet aroused the indignation of the Dalai Lama and his circle. Being out of reach of the ambans, they had made an attempt to obtain "the immediate protest" of the Russian government. This protest was to contain the demand, on behalf of the Dalai Lama, to abolish this convention and conclude a new one with the Dalai Lama's knowledge and consent, as well as to recall the amban from Lhasa. Such protest on the part of Russia, however, did not follow. It had to be not quite unexpected for the Tibetans, but nevertheless it had a dispiriting effect on them, as they had lost their last hope of opposing the convention.

"The heavy burden binding the will and decision of the high priest to return to Lhasa", Kuzminskiy wrote at that time from the

Russian consulate in Urga, "is the secrecy cloaking the recently concluded agreement on Tibetan affairs between England and China, as well as the mutual rights of the above-named powers in Tibet. Having received from dignitaries specially sent by the Chinese emperor much less information than was reported to him confidentially by Russia, which does not take part in the named treaty, and having substantial reasons to suspect that in the complete text of the treaty, stubbornly concealed from him by the Chinese government...and at least in the contents of those parts of the treaty that have been communicated to him, there is absolutely no information as to how England and China guarantee the inviolability of his person and protect his rights over Tibet that have been consecrated by time, the high priest is inclined to conclude that the English ignore his person as ruler, just as they did before."[39]

The reaction of the Dalai Lama to the Anglo-Chinese Convention of 1906 as an agreement, to a considerable extent binding for Tibet, was unerring. That is why the Ch'ing government, being one of the parties, exerted efforts to conceal its contents from the Dalai Lama. "Being very much surprised," Kuzminskiy continued, "by the caution of the Chinese dignitaries who dared not confirm in writing assertions about restoring the Dalai Lama to the rights of supreme ruler of Tibet that were repeatedly expressed in talks with the high priest...the Dalai Lama long ago began to hesitate in his decision made on the advice of our government to return to Lhasa immediately, not having at his disposal exact information about the agreement so strongly affecting his personal interests and the fortunes of his country."[40]

Staying in Mongolia, the Dalai Lama enjoyed immunity from the Ch'ing authorities. That is why they were trying to make him leave. Accordingly, the Ch'ing dignitaries sent to him "left no stone unturned to achieve the desired goal, making use of all possible means from flattery, unrealizable promises and requests to threats."

Such threats were also coming from the Ch'ing functionaries serving permanently in Mongolia during the entire period of the Dalai Lama's stay in Urga. "The local administration", the consul Kuzminskiy wrote, "cannot accept the fact of the high priest's staying close to the Russian borders. Out of fear of weakening his power in Mongolia, the amban in Urga declared that forcible measures would be undertaken against the high priest, if the latter will refuse to leave Mongolia." All this made it necessary to be on the alert. Even the Dalai Lama's adherents among the Mongolian princes recognized "the necessity to maintain good relations with China due to the impossibility of expecting Russian help in the nearest future and for lack of any other source of influential intercession."[41]

And indeed, St Petersburg was not encouraging hopes in this respect. At the end of February, 1906 Agvan Dorjiev had an audience with the Tsar. It had been promoted by Minister of Foreign Affairs Count V. N. Lamzdorf. Informing him about it, Dorjiev wrote: "Yesterday I was happy to be introduced to His Majesty, the Emperor, in Tsarskoye Selo. His Majesty, the Emperor, deigned to accept a personally written letter from the Dalai Lama and gifts from His Holiness." The audience was arranged at a high diplomatic level, solemnly, with its contents accurately fixed in writing by Dorjiev.

Addressing the Tsar and offering him the letter and presents, Dorjiev spoke on behalf of and on commission from his monarch: "His Holiness hopes that henceforth Your Majesty will also take to heart the interests of Tibet, the country connected by religious links with many of Your Majesty's subjects...His Holiness well realizes that only care for many other matters have, for the present, prevented Russia from expressing concern with Tibetan affairs to the extent that would be desirable for Russia. His Holiness has commissioned me to express once again his devotion to Your Majesty."[42]

The Tsar's answer was highly courteous, but did not contain any definite commitments or promises expected by Dorjiev. (It is to be supposed that Dorjiev was seeking an audience with the Tsar not for an interchange of politenesses.) It was said by way of reply: "Let me be believed that I, and Russia with me, are always ready to help Tibet in so much as we have power and resources. I hope, some time later, we shall render His Holiness an assistance even more potent and desirable for Tibet. Once again I repeat for His Holiness to believe me and always count on my good offices. I sincerely wish His Holiness good health in the kind governing of his country and for the benefit of Russia."[43]

In his record of the audience, Dorjiev apparently was not quite exact when reproducing the Tsar's words. It is doubtful whether the Tsar spoke about "more potent and desirable assistance" in such a non-concrete way and about the "benefit of Russia" (what had Russia to do with it?). The Tsar's position on the Tibetan matter was expressed much more exactly in the "Imperial Telegram of the Sovereign Emperor to His Holiness the Dalai Lama, the Supreme Head of the Tibetan People", in which there was no mention of any promises. The question was simply that the Buddhists who were Russian subjects have the opportunity to make pilgrimage to neighboring Mongolia in order to offer devotions to the Dalai Lama: "Rejoicing in the fact that my subjects may receive beneficial spiritual influence from Your Holiness, I ask you to believe my feeling of sincere gratitude and my respect for you."[44] The Dalai Lama, also in a telegraphic message, thanked the Tsar "for granting an audience to my representative Dorjiev and your highly gracious attention" to him, especially precious in such hard times for Tibet.[45]

The tenseness of the situation was due to the fact that Russian assistance was needed for a fundamental political restructuring of states in this part of Asia, which was to have serious repercussions. Preparations for it were being carried out in profound secrecy, which neither the Dalai Lama nor his adherents could entrust to letters or any other documents, however high their destination might be.

In the midsummer of 1906, Lieutenant-Colonel Khitrovo of general headquarters had presented to his chiefs detailed information on this matter, which has already been partly quoted above: "...Being guided exclusively by justice and meeting the needs and natural historical desires of a vast Lamaist flock, the Dalai Lama and his confederates—the Mongolian princes and influential khutughtu-gegens—have, in principle, irrevocably decided to separate from China and form an independent union, having realized this action under the patronage of and with support from Russia, thus avoiding bloodshed; and in case of Russia's refusal, to perform this action under the patronage of some other great power, even England in the last resort...The Russian support and patronage, in the Dalai Lama's opinion, should take the form of acknowledging the fair character of Tibetan and Mongolian lawful demands, accepting the Dalai Lama's representations on that matter and bringing them up for discussion and decision by all the great European powers..."[46]

A drastic enough historical turn in the restructuring of states by interested parties correspondingly demanded decisive, "drastic" executors. Khitrovo realized it very well, and that is why he considered it necessary to give a brief character sketch of the Tibetan ruler. "I consider it necessary to give some description of the Dalai Lama's personality. According to the vast information about him at my disposal, the common opinion from very different sources, without any exceptions, is that the present Dalai Lama represents an amazingly outstanding person. Starting from the 13th century, i.e. from the time of the first incarnation of the Dalai Lama, only one other of all the high priests (Ngawang Losang), who reigned at the beginning of the 17th century, was also prominent as an enterprising political figure...The present Dalai Lama is considered to be highly educated, with an innate outstanding intellect, invincible, persistent energy and tempered health. In the person of the Dalai Lama, the Mongolians see incarnate genius similar to that of the immortal Chingis Khan and the famous Khubilai Khan. Judging by his everyday way of life, the Dalai Lama is engrossed exclusively in persistent, stubborn, purely political activity, using his spiritual force in religion as a means for fulfilling his political tasks. He is extremely interested in European culture, desiring to become acquainted with it, starting from railroads...Even for his personal self, the Dalai Lama has commissioned Khambo Dorjiev to buy in St Petersburg the very best revolver. For his wintering, the Dalai Lama has built in Wang Hureng a small wooden house of Russian type, for which purpose Russian and Buryat carpenters have been engaged in Kyakhta, and the necessary materials have been bought...The extent to which the forthcoming events in Mongolia and Tibet may be important, provided the Dalai Lama will not be poisoned or killed, is obvious for anyone."[47]

This restructuring project, in its Tibetan part, could not be realized with the help of Russia, because the latter remained indifferent to such plans. As for "performing this action under the patronage of England in the last resort", this intention was even less realistic, since the balance of her relations with China and Tibet was initially and definitely not in favor of the latter. Besides, the Tibetans had a negative attitude towards her.

Khitrovo himself noted in his message: "One may judge about how persistent, consistent and independent the Dalai Lama is by his attitude towards the Chinese government and the English. The English repeatedly tried to get into correspondence with the Dalai Lama, but the Sovereign thus far returns English mail unopened."[48] As is generally known, from the very beginning of his rule as viceroy of India, Lord Curzon made substantial efforts to establish relations with Lhasa, but none of his letters were ever read there, having been returned unopened.

The Dalai Lama stayed in Urga for the entire year of 1907 as well, after which he left for Kokonor, where he resided on the way at a monastery at Wu-t'ai-shan. He called for Dorjiev to come there and soon gave him a new commission which, to fulfil, required his going to St Petersburg. Dorjiev brought with him a letter from the Dalai Lama to the Tsar and a *khadak* (ceremonial gift scarf).

On May 29, 1908, the Dalai Lama's messenger addressed the Russian foreign ministry with a written summary of his commission. Its first item was "to present the deep appreciation of His Holiness to the Sovereign Emperor for the highly gracious patronage of His Majesty in the happy settlement of the Tibetan matter marked by the Anglo-Russian Convention, and to present to His Majesty a sacred image of Buddha and a *khadak*, as a way to express the unlimited devotion of the Dalai Lama."[49]

Such a high appraisal given by Dorjiev and the Dalai Lama to the Anglo-Russian Convention of 1907 as "the happy settlement of the Tibetan matter" originated from scantiness of information about its contents. The request in the same summary "to hand to the Dalai Lama a certified copy of the Anglo-Russian Convention, possibly in Russian, English and Chinese languages" [50] speaks for this as well.

Presenting similar gifts to the Russian foreign minister, Dorjiev testified to him "the deep gratitude of the Dalai Lama in connection with the conclusion of the aforementioned convention recognizing the international status of Tibet." Subsequent first-hand acquaintance with a text of the convention might have disappointed the Tibetans with its clause on the recognition of Chinese suzerainty over Tibet, though that "suzerain" status was still more preferable for them than the former condition, which had not been qualified at all. Besides, resting upon this convention, the Dalai Lama had asked already "not to refuse to show the way for Tibet to achieve the complete evacuation of the English from the Valley", though there was practically no need for these directions since the occupation of the Chumbi Valley had already been terminated as an effect of obligations previously undertaken by the British party.

Considering that the convention had essentially improved the international status of Tibet, the Dalai Lama hurried to return there. The corresponding item can be found in Dorjiev's address: "Taking into consideration that the Chinese may, under various pretexts, delay an audience with the Chinese emperor in order to prevent the Dalai Lama from returning to Lhasa before long, His Holiness hopes for possible support in Peking on the part of the Russian government."[51] And finally, the summary included the invariable item: "To point out to the Dalai Lama what measures may be undertaken for the closer rapprochement of Tibet with Russia." Certainly, the government of Russia could not have any objections to the Dalai Lama's return to Lhasa, and the embassy in Peking was of the same opinion.

Besides the political issues, Dorjiev was to be engaged in practical affairs aimed at developing cultural ties between Russia and Tibet. He had been instructed to carry out personally both the presentations to His Majesty and one more commission, which was no less important. Namely, he was to ask for permission from the Russian government to construct a Buddhist temple in St Petersburg in order to satisfy the religious needs of the Russian Buddhists—Buryats, Kalmyks and others. The Dalai Lama had instructed him to buy for this temple a plot in St Petersburg and authorized him to spend 50,000 roubles for initial expenditures.

At the same time, he sent a request to the Russian government to admit Tibetan bursary students into various educational institutions in Russia, as well as to let Buryat specialists in electrical engineering, mechanical engineering, mining and similar disciplines come to Tibet to educate the Tibetans.[52]

Both tasks were difficult to fulfil. There were very few Buryat nationals who were technically educated specialists, and even fewer who wanted to go to Tibet. That is why the request to send those specialists had no results. As for the temple, it was constructed finally at the Dalai Lama's expense, though the very beginning of this undertaking seemed not so promising. The heads of the Russian orthodox church continuously laid obstacles to its construction in the capital of the state.

Although orthodoxy had been the state religion and one of the foundations of the state system (the official doctrine included the triad: autocracy, orthodoxy and national character), state policy had always been tolerant of different denominations and religions. It was not forbidden to build mosques and synagogues in the capital itself, and their existence in St Petersburg created the precedent for erecting a Buddhist temple there as well. However, the church authorities ("the long-haired Popes", according to Dorjiev's expression, as opposed to the shaven-headed Buddhist clergy) did not want to reconcile themselves with the construction of yet another heterodox temple in the city.

It was not without the efforts of the "long-haired" that the Russian foreign ministry reprimanded Dorjiev severely on account of the illegality of collecting money for building the temple among

Russian subjects in Russia itself. As a result, Dorjiev had to give explanations and proof that he was not collecting any means. In his autobiography, he notes that he then mentioned the enormous sum he had received from the Dalai Lama for that purpose. Orthodox authorities in their rage demanded that Dorjiev should be withdrawn from the capital, and that he should be completely deprived of the right of entry.

Later Dorjiev wrote that the letters rained down upon him containing threats to kill him and to ruin the temple. One cannot but see an exaggeration in these words, since murder and ravage, as far as one can remember, have never been an instrument of orthodoxy in its strife against heterodoxy, except perhaps those letters that have been written by obscure fringe elements, of which there is never a lack in any religion.

The Tsar's permission to build the temple did not remove all the obstacles, but it did allay and smooth away the conflict. In August, 1915 the Buddhist temple in St Petersburg was completed and inaugurated. It was not a common construction, but the largest Buddhist temple in Europe. The finest marble, bronze and gold gilding were used. Twenty lamas were attached to the temple. Being the initiator of its construction, Dorjiev attracted to it the attention of the most outstanding Russian orientalists—Radlov, Shcherbatskoy, Oldenburg, Roerich; and he bound all his further fortunes on it.

Meanwhile, the Dalai Lama in Wu-t'ai-shan was tormented with hesitations about the vaguenesses of the Anglo-Russian Convention and awaited an audience with the emperor. His stay in the monastery lasted for an entire year. Finally he received the emperor's invitation, and on September 28, 1908 His Holiness arrived in Peking by train. Here he was to face further trials. He resided at the same Hsi-huang monastery that had been built to the north of the capital for the first visit of a Dalai Lama at the beginning of the Ch'ing dynasty's rule in China. However, this time even mere politeness was not displayed towards him. He was treated like a subject who had committed an offence.

"The degraded hierarch has submitted to rites which humiliated his dignity and confirmed his vassalage."[53] He had been granted with a new title indicating, however intricate it was, that his status was that of a subject.[54] A decree was also issued that stated: "On return to Tibet, His Holiness must strictly follow the laws of his sovereign state of China. He must inform everyone about the kindness of the Chinese emperor's court. He must call upon the Tibetans to be obedient and to follow the path of high morals. He must follow the ancient rites, obey the amban and respectfully execute our will."[55]

The obedience of the spiritual ruler and his submissiveness to temporal authorities, executing the will, not of the emperor even, but of his representative, the amban, all constituted a demand contradictory to the whole of the Buddhist universe. It drastically changed the character of the interrelations between the Dalai Lamas and the Chinese emperors. The point that as a spiritual person, a monk is a figure equal to an emperor, was the pivot of the treatise written 1,500 years before by the founder of the first Chinese Buddhist school, Shih Huei-yüan, entitled "A Monk Should Not Show Respect Towards An Emperor" ("Sha-man Pu-ching Wang-chih Lun").[56] This canonical "lun" (treatise, sutra) was the basis of an alignment between temporal and spiritual spheres that had lasted all the past centuries, without in the least losing its significance. And the status of the Dalai Lama, including the 13th, was fully based on this thesis. The same prerogative was enjoyed even by less high-ranking hierarchs of the Buddhist church.

One event is known that happened during a solemn reception on the occasion of the enthronement of Emperor Nikolai the Second. The Nikolaevskiy Hall in the winter palace was filled. Among the guests of honor were representatives of the Buryat delegation. Nikolai the Second came in, and everyone knelt. Only two standing figures remained in the hall: the Tsar and the Buryat Lama Lubsan Sandan Tsidenov...The Buryat delegation had to pay a fine, and Tsidenov to explain why he had acted in such a manner. "The spiritual Tsar does not kneel to the worldly Tsar," was the answer. The incident was settled.

The independence of the spiritual Tsar was also stressed in Dorjiev's contacts with Russian officials. In his "Memorandum" of February 27, 1906, that is during the period of the most dramatic changes in fortune for the Dalai Lama, Dorjiev made a kind of "reprimand" to these figures: "...it should be very desirable if, in future, in written addresses of the emperor's government to the Dalai Lama, the words `Your Right Reverend' were not used, as it was in the last minister's letter to His Holiness. This is because the Dalai Lama, due to his high status in the Buddhist hierarchy, deserves the title corresponding in Christian terms to the Pope of the Roman Catholic Church, and not that of a bishop."[57]

This was the way it was in Russia, but in China things were different. And this difference constituted an additional basis of no small importance to the Dalai Lama's preferences and orientation in his foreign policy actions. The humiliations the Dalai Lama had experienced on the part of the Ch'ing emperor's authorities did not serve to improve Sino-Tibetan ties. An American envoy in Peking, who met him in those days, stressed when reporting on these meetings that the Dalai Lama's dignity had been extraordinarily affected by his stay in Peking, and that he was leaving with an increased enmity towards the Chinese. The envoy believed that the Dalai Lama would not assist the Chinese in their measures planned to govern Tibet as a Chinese province. He also expected serious complications for his friend the Dalai Lama.[58]

Chapter Ten

On a visit to the viceroy

After his return to Lhasa in December, 1909, the Dalai Lama did not stay there for long. Soon witnessing the excesses committed by the Chinese soldiers, he was compelled at the beginning of the next year to flee from the capital once more. The Dalai Lama thus began the years of his second exile, this time in India. There, however, everything was different. While staying in Mongolia, he had engaged in energetic activity to draw Russia into settling Tibetan problems, and the local authorities never hampered such efforts on his part. In India, however, when he tried to continue seeking Russian support, the colonial authorities began opposing his actions and even attempted to deprive him of any links with the external world.

His flight from Lhasa had been noticed immediately. A message was sent to Peking via the British telegraph that linked Tibet with India. It informed that "the Dalai Lama, without any warning, in secrecy, escaped from the city in an unknown direction on the night of the 30th of January. Measures have been ordered at once to undertake his return."[1] The amban Lien Yu proposed that volunteers from the Chinese garrison in Lhasa secure and present him with the Dalai Lama's head. Three hundred riders took off in pursuit, and soon a fight began in which the pursuers suffered serious losses.

The route of the Dalai Lama's flight passed through Phari, where a British trade agent stood with an armed escort. The Tibetans asked the agent to call bodyguards for the Dalai Lama from India by telegraph. The colonial authorities, however, had ordered to offer the Dalai Lama nothing more than a place to stay. As for guarding his life, the orders for the agent's escort were, in case of a clash between Tibetans and Chinese, not to become involved in fighting under any circumstances whatsoever.[2]

At the very border, in Yatong, the head of a small Chinese garrison (frontier post) asked the Dalai Lama not to cross the border, but to write a complete report on the events to the Manchu Ch'ing emperor and the amban in Lhasa. But the approach of the pursuers interrupted the short stop in Yatong, and the Dalai Lama rushed to cross the Indian frontier.

The inevitability of the flight from Lhasa was obvious. The only question was in which direction to run. Russian officers in Kashgar knew that a number of officials from the Manchu administration had been given the task of capturing the Dalai Lama, and that they had sent reconnaissance detachments for that purpose. A report was received from the consulate in Kashgar that read: "The local tao-t'ai has received information that the Dalai Lama has escaped in disguise and is making his way for Russia through Khotan and Yarkand."[3]

But the Dalai Lama had chosen another route and had informed Dorjiev about it in detail. The Ch'ing government, he wrote, "to prevent our possible departure to the north from the capital, has sent a detachment of several thousand soldiers in the direction of Nagchu. So, obviously, it will be impossible to steal through to the north (to Mongolia, as in 1904—N. K.) There remains only one possibility: reaching India and relying on the present friendly relations between Russia and England. If destiny happens to lead us to reach English territory, you must immediately present assertions of our deep and unwavering faithfulness to Russia before the government of Russia and explain the true circumstances that have prevented us from breaking through to the north, in the direction of Great Russia."[4]

Some time later, being already in India and expressing in a letter "our unwavering faithfulness to Russia", the Dalai Lama wrote to Dorjiev: "With special zeal, you should tell the high Russian government that I hope His Majesty's government already knows the conditions and events owing to the force of which I was compelled to make my way to India and not to the north, to Russia. May the high government believe me that my deep devotion to Russia has been pure and unwavering from the very beginning and shall remain so in future. It is exclusively due to the temporary conditions in which I find myself now that I cannot express my devotion in a more substantiating manner. At present, finding moral uplift in my being situated in the sacred land of India, I hope that, through the grace of the Supreme Buddha, I shall finally manage to lead my country out of its embarrassing situation with the assistance of Great Russia alone."[5]

Passing the original of the Dalai Lama's letter, with its translation, to the Russian foreign ministry, Dorjiev at the same time brought the contents of the Tibetan regent's message to the notice of governmental representatives. In this document, the situation was depicted somewhat allegorically: "To cure our country from temporary ailments that have befallen her, we have hitherto made all endeavors to rely on our customary physician (Russia); nonetheless, her ailments have been growing in strength. As before, we insistently beg you to take the most energetic measures that may cure the patient once and for all, and give her the possibility to live independently on her own, without subjection to the old poor physician (China)."[6] This time again, Dorjiev appended the original of the regent's letter to his translation.

On his own behalf, Dorjiev wrote to the Russian foreign minister: "His Holiness is far from thinking about reconciling himself to his present state of affairs. His Holiness turns his eyes towards Russia. It is my strong conviction that it depends only on Russia undertaking the appropriate steps there (in Tibet - N.K.) in order to consolidate His Holiness's position once and for all and save Tibet from being completely seized by China. This would have great moral significance for the prestige of Russia in the eyes of millions of Buddhists: Mongolians, Tibetans and others."[7]

There were numerous similar letters of appeal. Written in calligraphy on huge sheets of paper of distinctive Tibetan make, with large, bright red seals instead of signatures, they were courteous to the utmost and often touching and tragic in their unanswered calls for help. Dorjiev translated them all into Russian and passed them over to the Russian foreign ministry, even those that were not appeals, but instructions from the Dalai Lama to Dorjiev himself. Apparently in this way, Dorjiev sought to strengthen the government officials' confidence in him and win their favorable disposition towards his capacity as the Dalai Lama's messenger.

Dorjiev's role in Russia was extremely complex and rather difficult. His contribution to the establishment of friendly relations between Tibet and Russia has not been duly recognized as yet. And his role indeed had nothing to do with that of a spy or conspirator. In his "Memorandum on the Status of Tibet" presented to the Russian minister of foreign affairs in February, 1913 Dorjiev wrote: "In former times, I was considered an agent of the Russian government, a man who had been bribed by Russia to kindle enmity between Tibet and England. A high reward had been fixed for my capture, and I nearly fell into the hands of Indian police at the Nepalese border."[8]

The colonial authorities of British India hunted for Dorjiev. The circumstances of his departure on his second embassy to Russia were memorable to him. He and his party stole through to Colombo under the guise of being Nepalese pilgrims, while British policemen stopped them every now and then and demanded their documents. On his way back to Tibet, he did not even venture to travel by sea and across Indian territory, fearing for his life. Instead, he returned by way of the Mongolian steppes and deserts during the late autumn season when, due to bad weather, no ordinary caravans ever travelled. This journey took a very long time, and he reached Lhasa only after three months' travel.

But it was the Tsar who was least interested in Dorjiev; and, if we may still use the term, Dorjiev was rather the Dalai Lama's "agent" in Russia than the Tsar's "agent" in Tibet. True, he had not been officially recognized as the Dalai Lama's representative. The St Petersburg newspaper *Rech* wrote in those days: "The Russian government considers these letters (meaning the Dalai Lama's letters that Dorjiev was passing on to the foreign ministry—N.K.) to be a private correspondence, all the more so because it does not recognize Dorjiev as the Dalai Lama's representative. In Petersburg, Dorjiev is merely a representative for spiritual affairs for the Russian Buryats."[9]

Indeed, he was much occupied with religious matters, striving to build a Buddhist temple in St Petersburg. However, his main tasks were not religious but political issues, which he endeavored to solve in the name of the Dalai Lama. In this respect, the statement Dorjiev made at a meeting with the Russian foreign minister in March, 1910, was characteristic. "I assure you with confidence," he said, "that the deep devotion of His Holiness the Dalai Lama and the government of Tibet towards Russia will remain henceforth as well, and I apply once again for the intercession of Russia on behalf of His Holiness and the Tibetan government. The eyes of Tibet, which is experiencing hard times now, are fully turned in the direction of Russia. In the eyes of millions of Buddhists honoring the Dalai Lama and Tibet, it would be of the highest importance to Russia's prestige (for her) to exert influence on China, in one way or another, in order that the latter should stop its cruel policy in Tibet, cease the ravages, robberies, murders and desecration of sanctuaries being committed by the Chinese now, and finally, for the sake of science, put an end to the destruction and plundering of all things of historical value in Tibet. The Dalai Lama has directed his steps towards India because of the physical impossibility of fleeing to Russia."[10]

However, Dorjiev's unyielding indefatigability was fruitless. There was no evil intent behind this—the ministry leaders were just very reserved in their Tibetan policy. According to a record of the conversation that took place at Dorjiev's meeting on March 7, 1910, the minister answered in reply to Dorjiev's question that he had no exact information about events in Tibet, and thus he could not define the attitude of the Russian government towards those events. "Anyway," he said, "the Russian government continues treating the Dalai Lama with complete benevolence...Of course, it is impossible for Russia to take an active part in Tibetan affairs, but, having a benevolent attitude towards the Dalai Lama, the Russian government will not deprive him of its moral support." When asked by Dorjiev whether the Dalai Lama might be received by the Sovereign Emperor, the minister answered that "he would take this request into consideration and give him his answer later."[11]

Thus the position of Russia in Tibetan affairs was limited to the Dalai Lama's person. But even within the bounds of this narrow approach, St Petersburg officialdom was not binding itself with any obligations, alleging lack of information about Tibetan events.

Non-governmental bodies, on the other hand, spoke more unequivocally on the question. The newspaper *Rossiya* wrote in those days in connection with the Dalai Lama's flight ("this time not to the north, to the Russian borders, but south, across the Indian ones"): "Just say, for goodness' sake, what do we care for Tibet with its Dalai Lama? For, in order to display an active interest in it, one should have some rights or at least some exclusive real benefits that could justify such interference and such interest. But in this case, we have neither one nor the other."[12]

As a non-governmental body, the newspaper had the right to reason about the lack of rights or interests in Tibet. But the government had another point of view, because its status as a great power made it impossible to simply brush aside any events in any corner of the world. It was natural, then, that the Russian envoy to Peking visited the Chinese foreign ministry in February, 1910, where he made a statement, according to which "Russia cannot be indifferent to the destiny of the Dalai Lama, the spiritual head of numerous Russian Buddhists, and to such violations of the foundations of the Lamaist religion as could give rise to fermentation among our Buddhists."[13]

A report on the visit pointed out: "The dignitaries declared that China did not intend to change the internal structure of Tibet or undertake any restrictive measures with respect to lamaism."[14] Such an answer may be regarded only as a supercilious excuse and unwillingness to discuss the substance of the matter, because the previous years' actions of Chao Erh-feng, Ch'ang Yin-t'ang and other Ch'ing officials were directed exactly at changing the internal structure of Tibet. And as for the measures taken with respect to lamaism, it is impossible to call them "restrictive": they were barbarous. As Chinese sources state, "the dignitary Chao Erh-feng and detachment head Chung robbed property, killed population, burned down chapels, and put ecclesiastics to death in K'ang-pa district. They also melted down copper Buddha images for copper coins and mortar shells, as well as threw sacred Buddhist books into the dirt and dung, burned down over 1,000 chapels and private buildings, and killed over 1,100 monks and laymen."[15] And this was only the beginning.

Nevertheless, the Russian diplomatic corps did not try in any way to obtain a more intelligible answer. Proceeding from the fact that there were millions of Buddhists in Russia, for whom the Dalai Lama was the supreme religious authority, they pursued a Tibetan policy that limited their diplomatic interest within this frame, despite having the opportunity to solve the entire Tibetan problem at their own discretion with the consent of the Dalai Lama and his government.

One may suppose that pursuing a more active policy with respect to Tibet, not to mention rendering help and patronage to this country, threatened the Tsar's government with a serious increase in the Dalai Lama's prestige to the detriment of that of the Tsar. Although such consequences were, judging from appearances, never considered anywhere on the official level, they seem to be the most reasonable explanation for the government's refusal to take part in Tibetan affairs, despite it not requiring from Russia either financial expense, deployment of soldiers or the exertion of any particular diplomatic effort.

The Dalai Lama's representatives managed to contact the Russian consulate in Calcutta. Owing to this fact, the circumstances of the Dalai Lama's stay in British India became better known, despite the difficulty in maintaining communication with the consulate. The very first Russian consul to India, Klemm, wrote at this time: "The English authorities view us with extreme suspicion, and all members of the consulate are under constant and vigilant police surveillance. Letters and postal parcels bear signs of offhand unsealing. Specially commissioned detectives are filling whole volumes with notes about every trip of ours..."[16] Yet still the Dalai Lama's confidants maintained communication.

By the end of 1910, one of these confidants informed consulate representative Arseniev that "the Dalai Lama is distressed by the prison-like conditions the English have created for him. Not one foreigner may have access to him without special permission of Bell, who supervises him. They do not let him communicate with Tibet. Letters received or sent by him pass through the hands of English authorities. Isolated from the entire world, he is completely in the dark about events in his native country and about the current phase of Anglo-Chinese negotiations concerning his fate."[17]

By comparison, in the years of his first exile in Urga, the Dalai Lama regularly received reports from his agents based on foreign newspapers. At least once or twice a week, he received mail from Tibet, as well as reports from his agents in Peking. He thoroughly discussed, considered and summarized all this information in his decisions. The Dalai Lama sought permission to proceed to Calcutta to obtain an audience with the viceroy and learn something about his future lot. They told him that Lord Harding would be busy throughout that winter and would have no opportunity to receive him. Not directly forbidding him to go to Europe, Bell, pleading the difficulties and dangers of travelling by sea, persistently advised the Dalai Lama not to undertake such a distant journey.

"Not having any particular hopes that London will display more sympathy to his bitter fate than Calcutta, he sets all his expectations on an intercession by the Russian government. In the meantime, he would like to live not on English territory, where everything is alien to him, but in Russia, for which he has always felt sincere friendship and deep affection."[18]

At the beginning of April, the newspaper *Sankt-Peterburgskiye Vedomosti* reported that in the near future the Dalai Lama, who resided in exile in India, was going to travel to Europe by sea, so that he might visit his devotees in Russia. Other newspapers also wrote about it later. However, the colonial authorities kept a tenacious hold on the Dalai Lama, and the above-mentioned journey never took place.

The negative British attitude towards the Tibetans compelled the latter to address the Russian government over and again. At the end of December, 1910, the Russian consulate in Calcutta reported that a confidant of the Dalai Lama had asked for a swift reply whether or not the Dalai Lama might count on support from the Russian government, and what would it think about his coming to Russia from London, where he was going to travel.[19] The Dalai Lama's intention to seek support in Europe, and primarily in Russia, had remained immutable from the very start of his exile. It had become especially strong after the fruitless Sino-Tibetan negotiations in September.

Yet there was no hopeful news from St Petersburg. In March, 1911, Prince F. I. Shcherbatskoy returned from his journey to India and brought Dorjiev the Dalai Lama's letter to the Tsar. The Dalai Lama wrote in it: "From the moment when friendly relations were established between Russia and Tibet, we, remembering your admonition exactly, have maintained most peaceful and loyal decorum, with obedience and respect, towards the Chinese up until the end. But despite this, the Chinese have taken away all rights from Tibet and have driven us into the condition in which we, the head of the country, with our retainers, are deprived of the opportunity to remain in our land...It is impossible to watch passively what is being done daily by the Chinese in Tibet."[20]

In his letter, the Dalai Lama proposed contacting the British government and making, together or separately, representation about this matter to the Chinese government. If it became necessary, he also suggested referring the matter for international consideration. His other proposal was for the Tibetans to address some other government which, in the opinion of the government of Russia, would be most suitable for this purpose. The Dalai Lama himself was ready to come to St Petersburg, if St Petersburg agreed. In conclusion, he said: "We turn to your intercession in order that the country might be rid of the Chinese and become free."[21]

The high-ranking Tibetans attached to the Dalai Lama in Darjeeling also sent a letter full of anxiety about Tibet's future. Since the Chinese "are intending to deprive the Dalai Lama of temporal power, to subordinate the Tibetans completely, to place Chinese rulers everywhere, to station Chinese troops, to seize all lands and waters, and so on, in a word, to destroy our religion and state...it is necessary that Tibet exist as an independent nation, without fear of capture, either by China or England."[22] The mail brought by Shcherbatskoy included detailed instructions from the Dalai Lama for Dorjiev concerning ways of realizing the task he had been set, and ended with the words: "For the sake of truth and virtue, you must keep in the depth of your heart that you, as before, will direct all your diligence and wit to finding wise means for resolving our cause."[23]

There were no serious divergences of view, in St Petersburg, concerning Tibet at the various levels of foreign policy management. In the process of preparing the Tsar's answer to the Dalai Lama, a memorandum was presented that recommended giving a reassuring answer, but necessarily confining it to possibly only more general expressions, "so that exaggerated hopes might not be aroused".[24]

The Tsar's actual letter was not only reserved and reassuring, as had been recommended in the memorandum, but edifying as well. The Tsar added a maxim in favor of England: "I consider following a policy of consent in Tibetan affairs with the Great British government to be one of the important conditions...for the most swift and happy solution of the present confusing situation."[25]

Throughout the time that the Dalai Lama was proceeding from Peking to Lhasa and then, after a short stay in his capital, going into exile in India, Dorjiev remained in St Petersburg. But there were no interruptions in communication between them thanks to special messengers sent by the Dalai Lama from India, despite all the difficulties in organizing their travels. Finally, after three years' stay in St Petersburg, Dorjiev was to go to the Dalai Lama in answer to a summons by His Holiness.

Before his forthcoming departure, Dorjiev sent a detailed letter to the Russian ministry for foreign affairs, in which he set forth his views on the correlation between the forces and interests of each of the parties involved in Tibetan affairs, as well as outlined some prospects for finding a solution to the situation. He stated in his letter that, in view of Tibet's remoteness, Russia did not recognize any presence of her political and economic interests there. Her interests were purely religious, and concerned only the Russian Buddhists. At the same time, the author noted, Britain's interests were mostly political. From this, he concluded that Tibet's foreign policy must be based on a foundation of friendliness and peace with Great Britain. It would be necessary to come into various agreements of a political and economic nature with her.

Traditional ways of thinking, Dorjiev continued, were rather strong in the Tibetan people, with their patriarchal way of life. Having once taken root, their ideals, traditions and sympathies, as well as their antipathies and estrangements, become set and yield to outside influence only with great difficulty. The long-standing benevolent attitude of Russia towards Tibet, which had been proven more than once in reality and confirmed in writing, has caused all Tibetans, regardless of class distinction, to believe that Tibet's protection from her grasping neighbors would come from the direction of Russia. This faith had struck a deep root in all Tibetan people and was mystically haloed.

On the other hand, the Boer campaign, Younghusband's expedition and riots in neighboring India have strongly impressed the minds of both educated Tibetans and the lower strata of Tibetan society. A prejudice against the British has acquired an historical coloring and has become fixed in the people's consciousness.

Living in St Petersburg for many years and observing the growing Anglo-Russian mutual understanding within the limits of the Entente, Dorjiev nevertheless had the courage to counterpoise these countries one against the other—so different were they, he stressed, in the eyes of the Tibetans.

Further in his letter, Dorjiev set forth, without ceremony, his intentions to cultivate an Anglophile attitude of mind in Tibet after his return there. "Apparently, my task in Tibet will be, together with His Holiness the Dalai Lama, to try to annul the strictly opposite aspirations and feelings of the Tibetans, and convince them of the necessity of holding a loyal attitude towards the English—that is to say, to destroy what has been created before. This is a highly difficult task. Even the tremendous prestige of the Dalai Lama cannot neutralize (the feelings of) the people at large. (Even if we succeed, the danger is that) this may lead the Tibetans to the perilous assumption that Russia has ostensibly left Tibet to the absolute arbitrariness of England for some concessions."[26]

Here, Dorjiev intrudes into the field of Anglo-Russian relations. As for the Tibetan policies of these two countries, modern historians, both foreign and native, have viewed this aspect of their relations on the basis of the undoubtedly false conviction that Tibet served for Russia as a means of achieving British concessions, even if they granted that it had not been an object of her territorial expansion.

True, in official correspondence it sometimes was suggested to use the Tibetan factor in dealings with Britain. Thus Nabokov, the Russian consul to India, imitating, consciously or not, the British functionaries' methods of conducting the diplomatic game due to his regular contacts with them, wrote: "If I may be permitted to express my personal opinion, the time has come, one would think, finally to arrange things with England and, maybe by dint of recognizing her primary interests in Tibet, to obtain satisfaction of more urgent political benefits in other spheres, where our interests come in touch with the English ones."[27]

Co-operation between the British and Chinese governments in Tibetan affairs and in their relations with Russia at the time of the Russo-Japanese War (of 1904-05) gave grounds for Khitrovo, the head of the Russian expedition to Mongolia, to note the positive role of the Dalai Lama during that period. Nevertheless, in what was similar to that indisputable occasion, Khitrovo did not suggest using him in the capacity of an object around whom to make Anglo-Russian deals. "I dare not judge whether or not the Dalai Lama may be useful for us, the Russians, but I know and firmly report the one thing I am aware of: during the war, the Mongolians all ignored the Chinese government's orders not to sell cattle and horses to the Russians thanks exclusively to the Dalai Lama."[28]

There is not a single document that can bear witness to the approval of some proposal to use the Tibetan problem to the benefit of the Russian government. Besides, Britain was seeking "to finalize an agreement" concerning Tibet with the Ch'ing authorities and to build her relations with Russia according to the results of this arrangement. No author, alleging that Russia used Tibetan problems to her benefit, has ever adduced any data in favor of this claim. Dorjiev spent many years near the kitchen of Russian foreign policy and so his knowledge of the true state of affairs in detail gave him grounds to deny "that Russia left Tibet to the absolute arbitrariness of England ostensibly for some concessions."

In his letter to the Russian foreign ministry, Dorjiev, foreseeing difficulty in filling the Tibetans with loyalty to Britain, assumed the possibility of achieving the totally opposite results: "There is but a single step from here to constant sharp opposition to England, or to something even worse (possibly, opposition to Russia herself—N.K.)." To avoid this, Dorjiev returned to the idea of a Russian involvement in Tibetan affairs, even if jointly with Britain which, in his opinion, would not be too burdensome for Russia. "According to my deep conviction," his letter read, "the above-stated and highly possible complications might be successfully paralyzed by establishing the joint patronage of Russia and England over Tibet, based on one or another contractual agreement...This measure may completely assuage the public opinion of Tibet and bring about the desired results. The presence of both

Russian and English representatives in Lhasa might inspire conviction in the Tibetans not to fear any forceful measures."[29]

Having addressed the Russian government for many years and not having received any Russian help in solving Tibetan problems, the Tibetans started to make plans for a joint Anglo-Russian protectorate over their country, as can be seen from Dorjiev's letter. Russian participation in such a protectorate could dampen the "sharp opposition to England" in Tibet, since the Tibetans regarded the former participant as a guarantor of goodwill. Besides, in this way the Tibetans expected to disrupt the unity of British and Chinese actions against their country, that had existed over the past seven years.

In view of these plans, the Dalai Lama's behavior during the period of his stay in India becomes clear. Having found himself in the position of being a captive of the British colonial authorities, who might deliver him at any time into Ch'ing hands, he nevertheless tried to avoid straining relations with them as the possible future ally of Russia in this planned joint protectorate.

The Russian diplomatic corps, however, was extremely far from planning any protectorate over Tibet. At the same time, they did not make a secret out of the interchange of letters between the Dalai Lama and the Tsar, nor out of the contents of those letters. The ambassador of Russia in London, Benckendorff, in December, 1911 informed Foreign Minister Grey that the Tsar was going to answer the Dalai Lama in general, "non-political" terms. Since the Dalai Lama was on Indian territory, the assistance of British authorities was necessary to pass the letter to its addressee.

The British party tried to delay as much as possible delivery of the letter, which took place only a few months later. Russian Consul Revelioti noted in his message to Deputy Foreign Minister Neratov that, having received the order to pass on the letter, "I had immediately informed Sir Henry McMahon, Secretary for Foreign Affairs of the Indian government, about my intention to visit the Dalai Lama and report to him the contents of what had been sent to me. Sir Henry promised to notify at once the political agent of Sikkim, Bell, of my arrival in Darjeeling, and apparently he had no objections to my meeting with the Dalai Lama. However, half an hour before my departure for Darjeeling, I received a letter from Under-secretary for Foreign Affairs Wood (i.e. McMahon's assistant—N.K.), who asked me to delay my journey for a few days, because it was unknown where the Dalai Lama was, and also in view of the absence of Mr. Bell, who had gone to Gangtok situated at a distance of three days' journey on mule from Darjeeling.

"Knowing for certain that the Dalai Lama did not leave his residence," the consul continued, "I answered Wood that I preferred to wait for Mr. Bell's return in Darjeeling...My information about the Dalai Lama's whereabouts proved to be correct. If I had fulfilled Wood's request and delayed my departure for several days, I could hardly have managed to hand the letter to the Dalai Lama, which is, to all appearances, what the local government had expected."[30]

Revelioti's visit to the Dalai Lama was just a protocol one. However, the Dalai Lama had tried to use it for his more important purposes: "delving into questions concerned with upholding Tibet's independence", according to Revelioti. In this connection, the Russian consul asked an interpreter to say that his visit "by no means had the character of a political mission and consisted only in delivering the letter, and that thus it would be difficult to say something definite about a joint policy with England concerning Tibet."[31]

After the procedure of presenting the letter was completed, the Dalai Lama's ministers expressed their wish to speak to Revelioti separately. But this attempt was undermined by Bell. In his report to Harding, he wrote, "I judged that the courtesy due to a representative of the Russian government required my presence at this interview also." Under such conditions, the Tibetan ministers could merely inquire about the possibility of a joint Anglo-Russian discussion of Tibet's future.[32]

Summing up the results of this meeting with the Dalai Lama, the consul reported that he had followed to the letter the strict procedures prescribed to him by the ministry and had stressed the absence of any political nature in the task with which he had been entrusted. At the same time, he remarked that "it would be very useful, in terms of the future, to maintain the hope of our care in these people who are far from alien to us. Our prestige in Tibet is high, while the proximity of Tibet to India, populated" in his opinion, "with timid and defenceless Indians, cannot be conducive to the idea of British grandeur among the Tibetans, who view the British supremacy in this country from a close distance. Consciousness of the fact that in Russia they do not forget about the Tibetan people's destiny constitutes for these people a much stronger moral support than the 1,000 rupees a month that the government of India presents to the deposed spiritual sovereign of Tibet."

As for the Dalai Lama's status, in the first place Revelioti noted, "The Tibetan high priest, who never sympathized with the English, is compelled to reckon with them against his will, being on the one hand their subsidized guest, not to say captive, and on the other, someone pressed by their promises of support, albeit rather vague promises."[33]

While the Xin-hai Revolution of 1911 overthrowing the Ch'ing emperor's regime with its bureaucratic state system was growing imminent in China, something quite contrary was happening in Tibet. The power of the Ch'ing officials in Lhasa was now at its height, and the excesses of the Chinese soldiers in abuse of the Tibetans were boundless. The Dalai Lama's absence plus the Chinese soldiers' support gave the amban Lien Yu an opportunity to attain to a power more absolute than the ambans had ever possessed before. Moreover, that power was used not for governing the country properly, but for personal mercenary purposes, and mostly to prove to the Tibetans that they were nonentities. For example, Lien Yu arrogantly humiliated the Tibetans, for his own pleasure, by introducing the order that even the highest Tibetan officials were to kneel in his presence. As Russian diplomats informed about Tibetan events noted, "The population has repeatedly submitted collective petitions (of protest) to Lien Yu, but he never pays the slightest attention to them."[34]

The same is witnessed by Chinese sources. When rendering the circumstances of the Tibetan break with China, Se Pin stated quite firmly, though mildly, that when Lien Yu "settled down in Lhasa as amban, he started to base his actions in his relations with the Tibetans on threats and fear, not on peaceful terms."[35] Thus arbitrariness, lawlessness, robbery and excesses committed by Chinese officials and soldiers constituted the gloomiest pages of Sino-Tibetan relations, casting a sombre shadow over their further development.

As has been mentioned, the government of China made no secret of its intention to turn Tibet into a Chinese province. Later, in fact, after the Xin-hai Revolution of 1911, the nationalist Chinese government formed the administrative unit "the Frontier District Ch'uan-pien" out of the eastern part of Tibet. After 10 more years, in 1924, they renamed it part of Szechuan province, which never was the case before, as this district had previously been governed from Lhasa.

The Xin-hai Revolution of 1911 gave a new impulse to anti-

Chinese actions in Tibet. It produced a debilitating effect on the Chinese soldiers fighting there, which was supplemented by their weariness from countless clashes with the Tibetans, being badly maintained in outfits, food and money, their isolation from their homeland, and similar factors. A British trade agent in Gyangtse noted "the growing unruliness of the Chinese soldiers", who had become completely out of hand. Even Chinese officials, both civil and military, were afraid of their soldiers and hurried to escape to China through Indian territory.

As a result of the soldiers' excesses, a long smouldering revolt broke out in Lhasa. The Chinese garrison under the command of Chung Ying dwindled away. Finally Chung Ying completely lost all control of events, and only his personal bodyguards were left obeying him. Other soldiers in different parts of the city were fending for themselves. Sino-Tibetan negotiations began, but were interrupted now and then by recommenced fighting.

In the middle of 1912, the president of the Chinese Republic, Yüan Shih-k'ai, asked the government of British India to assist in evacuating the remainder of the Chinese troops in Tibet. In September, a British mission was established on the Tibeto-Sikkim border for repatriating the Chinese. More than 2,000 soldiers had passed through the mission by March of the next year. The Russian consul in Calcutta reported: "The last remainder of.Chinese troops, representing a mob of wretched ragamuffins, in which one cannot possibly recognize soldiers, have been chucked out from Calcutta the other day."[36] Not a departure, but a "chuck out", was due to their turbulent behavior causing numerous troubles for the police.

Later, in one of his letters to St Petersburg, Dorjiev wrote that when he came to Lhasa it looked like a heap of ruins. According to the Dalai Lama's order, it was forbidden to slaughter the rest of the Chinese. They were to be sent in parties to the Indian border, from where they would be forwarded to China through Calcutta by sea.[37]

Up to the very last moment, Yüan Shih-k'ai feigned that nothing particular was happening in Tibet. Everything was taking its normal course and the old Ch'ing order was to be preserved. Chung Ying was told to stay on in Lhasa. But when all his soldiers scattered, he had no alternative but to leave the city. Nepalese guards escorted him on his way to the Indian border. In the Chumbi Valley, he attempted to hang himself in the local custom-house, out of a fit of despair. On return to Peking, he was arrested, prosecuted and beheaded on presidential decree for having left Tibet.

The subsequent relations of being neighboring states stabilized between China and Tibet. As the Chinese historian Hua Ts'e-yu put it at the beginning of the 1930s, it was based on the indisputable fact that "the Chinese troops quartered in Tibet were defeated, and the Dalai Lama has returned to Lhasa and proclaimed the independence of Tibet."[38]

Nevertheless, starting from the first president of the Republic, Yüan Shih-k'ai, and during all 40 years of nationalist rule in China, attempts continued to restore relations between Peking and Lhasa to a state similar to the old one. At times, those attempts looked miserable and tragi-comic, but the Kuomintang government had no other means for establishing this.

Some Chinese historians have appraised the political course of Peking objectively, stating that impotent, corrupt, reactionary rulers were invariably pursuing a policy of Chinese nationalism, oppression and dissidence with respect to Tibet. Just like the Ch'ing government, they adhered to a reactionary policy with respect to national minorities, making use of local cut-throat detachments (obviously, numerous Chinese militarists of the 1920s and 30s are meant, who had their own military formations—N.K.), and acting with lies and fraud. They aimed at parcelling out the Tibetan nation in order to spread their supremacy over the Tibetans.[39]

Chapter Eleven

"If only it is done sub rosa"

The fall of the Ch'ing dynasty in China as a result of the Xin-hai Revolution of 1911 coincided with a radical turn in the development of events in Tibet. Prospects for the Dalai Lama's return to Tibet and his restoration to power there began to show. The traditionally close Tibeto-Mongolian ties caused aspirations for independence in Mongolia to strengthen as well. Regardless of any Russian or British plans for central Asia, the Tibeto-Mongolian region was maturing for separation from China.

On the eve of these drastic changes, the Ch'ing military-bureaucratic regime was looking for external enemies to explain the devolvement of the empire towards its collapse. The Russian newspaper *Rech* wrote that the amban in Lhasa "reported to Peking, `The Russians are provoking a Lamaist riot in Tibet and Mongolia'."[1]

Dorjiev immediately responded to this newspaper report. "By what means and through whom," he asked as a rhetorical question in his letter to the Russian foreign ministry, "could Russia pursue her projects now, such as provoking a riot among the Lamas? It may be assumed, with high probability, that China has the evil intention to recognize as political agents of Russia the Russian Buddhist subjects staying in Tibetan monasteries, as well as Russian pilgrims, so that, based on this, she can stop Russian contacts with Tibet undesirable for her..."[2]

It is useless to deny that Russia took part in establishing independence in Mongolia. But her participation never took the shape of intrigue or armed invasion. "The Russian threat" existed to an even lesser degree in Tibet acquiring her independence, which was the cherished goal of the Dalai Lama. If such a threat were real, the British party could easily have avoided it by merely not losing its hold on the Dalai Lama. His two years of actual captivity could have been turned into three, five or more without difficulty. However, there were no obstacles of such a nature. The Ch'ing authorities, with whom its mutual understanding had existed, were dethroned, while the new power in China did not as yet show its loyalty to Britain clearly enough. So the Dalai Lama was set free.

Dorjiev's reunion with the Dalai Lama, due to take place in

1911, was delayed because of the indefinite situation in China resulting from the Xin-hai Revolution. Concerning this, Dorjiev wrote to the Russian minister for foreign affairs that His Holiness the Dalai Lama is deeply worried over what is happening, and feels anxious about Tibet, "which is in many respects connected with Mongolia. Tibet's proximity to India makes the Dalai Lama alarmed over the possibility of an occupation of his country by the English in case of further complications in China. The question arises, whether it will be recognized as possible to save Tibet from complete abolition of her independence by means of some negotiations now, while the situation is still indefinite. As long as the Russian state has interests in neighboring Mongolia, Tibet's destiny cannot be indifferent to the Russian government."[3] Thus did Dorjiev push the Russian government to act in favour of Tibet, while he himself already was sitting on his trunks about to depart from St Petersburg, where he had settled down rather thoroughly by that time.

The return address on Dorjiev's letter was "St Petersburg, Staraya Derevnia, the Buddhist Temple", where he stayed on for some time more while its construction continued, corresponding further with Russian officials. He asked the latter to give him an armed escort, since his planned route through Mongolian territory "lies across country with an outlaw population". Though the route by sea and through India was faster and more reliable, Dorjiev was more apprehensive of the British authorities than "an outlaw population".

Leaving Russia, he did not sever his links with her. In his official correspondence, Dorjiev explained that he was not going because his goal was unachievable: "In view of the imminence of important changes in the inner structure of the Chinese empire, the Dalai Lama has now decided to return to his throne. In his last letters, he asks me to proceed to Tibet immediately...If the Russian government shares the opinion that it would be desirable to maintain the feelings of faith and friendship that the Tibetan people entertain towards Russia, I request it to indicate to me which mode of behavior I should follow in Tibet."

Dorjiev's preparations for departure were not a secret. But they became protracted and the colonial authorities in India displayed their impatience with this delay. In the middle of June, news came from the Russian consulate in Calcutta that one of the local newspapers had published an article dealing with this matter, which read: "The intransigent Dorjiev is still active. Latest rumors have it that in Petersburg he keeps on pretending to be the Dalai Lama's agent; and Russian diplomats are clever enough to take advantage of the Tibetans' mistakes and force concessions out of Great Britain in other fields, even if they do not deal with Tibet directly."[4]

The groundlessness of such assumptions and accusations was obvious. Nevertheless, the anti-Russian strain in Indian newspapers was not getting any weaker. A message from the Russian consul, received in St Petersburg after Dorjiev's arrival in Tibet, noted that "organs of the local press, whose tenor is fear of `Russian intrigues' in Tibet, fall into an hysterical tone at the slightest hint of Dorjiev's presence in the camp of the Dalai Lama or, in general, at any indication of his contacts with Russia."[5]

The unseemly tone of newspapers lapsing into hysterics in connection with Dorjiev and Russia shared nothing in common with the realistic appraisal of Dorjiev's role that was given in secret correspondence by the British colonial administration. A British trade agent in Yatung reported to the state secretary for foreign affairs of the viceroy's government in July, 1912, that Dorjiev was waiting in Phari to meet the Dalai Lama on his way back to Lhasa, and that this meant the probability of the Dalai Lama pursuing an independent foreign policy on his return home.[6]

But British colonial authorities did not mean to lose their control over the march of events. The Russian consul wrote from Simla, where the viceroy's government went in summer: "Though I do not have direct indications of this, it seems obvious to me that agents of the local government will be on the alert for the Dalai Lama's actions, and will not be too keen to encourage his movement from Gyangtse to a place where it would be much more difficult to carry out surveillance over him."[7]

Staying in Darjeeling by the Tibetan border for a long time, the Dalai Lama was restricted in his links with the outside world. This most probably was the reason why one of his letters to Russia was delivered in English translation:

> "To His Majesty, the Emperor of Russia:
> Your Majesty,
> I am most thankful to receive Your Majesty's kind letter and *khadak* (silk scarf) at Darjeeling from the Russian Counsellor to Calcutta. Your Majesty has been so kind and helpful to the religious and secular powers of Tibet, for which I am ever grateful. At present, myself being in British India, I am

consulting about Tibétan affairs also with the British government.

I beg to state to Your Majesty that ever since we have been furnished with a treaty, we have been strictly observing the conditions laid down in it, whereas the Chinese troops in Tibet have been quite contrary and have been dealing with the Tibetans very rudely.

I, therefore, request the favour of Your Majesty to kindly refer to the treaty and direct the Chinese troops in Tibet to conduct themselves according to its conditions agreed upon by both the Russian and British powers, and therefore to evacuate themselves from the country as soon as possible, leaving it independent under me.

I remain Your Majesty's true priest,
Dalai Lama
Kalimpong, Darjeeling Camp India
The 14th of February, 1912"[8]

The Dalai Lama also had no proper communication with Lhasa or Tibet in general, since the British authorities forbade him to be in correspondence. Only a few of his letters and, at that, only those in code, were received by the authorities in Lhasa. Lack of information from Tibet made him not hasty in returning home. Finally, however, when he had overcome all doubts about his safety, the Dalai Lama crossed the Tibetan border.

Dorjiev had set forth much earlier from Mongolia to meet the Dalai Lama. In Tsaidam, Dorjiev learned that fighting was still going on in Lhasa. However, that did not stop him. Having arrived at Phari, he sent letters and telegrams to the Dalai Lama, informing the latter of his arrival. Soon they met on Tibetan territory at Samding, four days' march from Lhasa. There, in Samding, and later in Lhasa, the Dalai Lama handed to Dorjiev 50,000 silver coins for the construction of the temple in St Petersburg. Precious gifts were also collected to be delivered in St Petersburg to the Tsar and his ministers.

The stop at Samding turned out to be a prolonged one, because fights in Lhasa continued. Later, the Dalai Lama halted for the same reason seven kilometers away from the city and stayed there until the end of the year. Only at the very end of 1912 could he return to the Potala. By that time, Dorjiev had already left him and gone north, to Mongolia and beyond, with new missions.

Meanwhile, Mongolia's independence had been accomplished, revealing itself in the formal enthronement of a native sovereign. The Dalai Lama sent a delegation to conclude a treaty. The Tibetan delegation was headed by Dorjiev, while negotiations on the side of Mongolia were conducted by the great Lama Rabdan who was, at the time, performing the duties of foreign minister. The negotiations were not disregarded by the press. The newspaper *Novoye Vremya* wrote: "Dorjiev is now in Urga where he has declared Tibet's independence and his powers to conclude a treaty between Tibet and Mongolia."[9]

At the very beginning of January, Chinese newspapers published information concerning the Tibeto-Mongolian negotiations. *Shun-ch'in Ribao*, distorting the truth just as the English newspapers did, pointed at Russia as the real cause of Tibet's aspiration for independence: "It is possible that now that Dorjiev has arrived in Urga, he will begin negotiations with the Russians, so that Tibet, like Urga, might proclaim her independence."

Be this as it may, the materials published by the newspaper were, in fact, indicative of the Tibeto-Mongolian negotiations, although not of Tibeto-Russian ones: "Urga and Tibet, acting in accord with each other, evidently display their wish to separate from China. The Chinese amban in Lhasa is unable to restore the lost power and significance of China in Tibet. Tibetan troops treat the Chinese army with contempt and disrespect, and it might not be possible to eradicate this Sino-Tibetan conflict. Lhasa occupies a protected position and fears nothing. The fact that Tibet has proclaimed independence, and the Dalai Lama has acceded to the throne, indicates that the Tibetans have overrated their own strength. But if Tibet establishes contacts with Urga, then who stands behind her?"[10]

The undisguised threat to Tibet "overrating her strength" and hints about those who allegedly stand behind her, served as a leitmotif for the Chinese press. British newspapers also repeated it. At the beginning of January, the Russian consul in Calcutta reported to St Petersburg: "The local English press has not been slow in responding to the news that Dorjiev is in Urga, and that he has announced Tibet's independence and declared his powers to conclude a treaty between Tibet and Mongolia.

"The *Daily Telegraph* has reprinted a dispatch from Peking stating that the Chinese government is fully aware and absolutely sure that each step of the Dalai Lama during the last few months has been undertaken in concordance with Russian agents in Urga...

"I have every reason to believe that the following editorial comment from the *Pioneer* newspaper reflects the Indian government's point of view on the Tibetan problem: "Last events have shown that it will be very difficult to settle this question," the *Pioneer* has written, meaning the settlement of the problem with the participation of Russia, as was sought by Dorjiev. "This cannot be allowed by either England or China. Our two governments prefer to discuss the issues concerning Tibet without outside interference." It seems beyond doubt to me that England does not want to lose the chance to reserve for herself a predominant position over what is happening in Tibet."[11]

The very first publications of the Tibeto-Mongolian Treaty aroused a distinctly negative reaction to it on the part of opponents of an independent Tibet that had allegedly taken her cue from Russia. According to Sir Charles Bell, "This `treaty' was concluded on behalf of Tibet by the Russian Buriat, Dorjieff, tireless as ever in the work of drawing Russia and Tibet together. His authority was based on a letter given him by the Dalai Lama, when the latter was fleeing from the British expedition to Lhasa. But the Dalai Lama denied that his letter—which enjoined Dorjieff to work for the Buddhist religion, a not uncommon request—justified anything in the nature of a treaty."[12]

There are no reasons for doubting Dorjiev's powers. Dorjiev was the only foreign representative of the Dalai Lama and had the authority to act on behalf of His Holiness. Dorjiev's correspondence with the Dalai Lama and with Russian officials indicates that he enjoyed the Dalai Lama's total confidence for many years and had high official status in Tibet, which allowed him to carry out negotiations of national importance and to sign corresponding documents.

The Tibeto-Mongolian Treaty on mutual recognition of independence by both parties, concluded by Dorjiev, befittingly crowned his selfless activity as a diplomat and an outstanding political figure in the field of Tibetan statehood. Dorjiev, however, did not consider the conclusion of the treaty to be his personal achievement, as can be understood from his comments on this matter during his meeting with the Russian consul in Urga.

This very consul wrote to St Petersburg in his report on the conclusion of the Tibeto-Mongolian agreement: "Handing me the tenor of this document, Dorjiev explained that the initiative for this agreement had come from the Dalai Lama (sic!—N.K.), who always sought to achieve spiritual and political unification of the two co-religionist and like-minded countries, similarly burdened by Chinese supremacy. The separation of Mongolia from China and the proclamation of the Khutughtu as Khan had made this aspiration of the Tibetan high priest stronger still. It had suggested to him the idea to give form to the planned rapprochement with a written agreement that made their mutual recognition of independence the foundation for it.

"The Dalai Lama's proposal received a sympathetic welcome at Urga, where the text of the agreement was then drawn up in accordance with directives received by Dorjiev and the desires of the Mongolians, who used the Treaty of the 21st of October as a pattern...The Khutughtu, who stands lower in the spiritual hierarchy, could not but be flattered by the proposal to conclude the agreement—moreover, an agreement on equal terms—that came from the Tibetan reincarnate whose authority in matters of faith is considered peremptory...

"The rapprochement of Tibet and Mongolia will make an even more unfavorable impression in Peking because the well-known, ancient rivalry between the Dalai Lama and the Khutughtu, which sometimes had a rather sharp character, had been supported by China. This rivalry, one should hope, is now eliminated for the sake of the more important common goal—the national unification of the two kindred peoples and their mutual assistance against Chinese domination."[13]

In fulfilment of its commitments, the Russian foreign ministry acquainted the British ambassador to St Petersburg with the contents of the treaty and the Russian consul's telegram about its conclusion immediately after the receipt of the documents. As the consul had expected, the Tibeto-Mongolian rapprochement did produce an unfavorable impression, but its impact was far beyond his expectations. Yüan Shih-k'ai's regime was more preoccupied with its home affairs. British imperialism, however, did not wish to let the development of world events slip out of its hands. This rapprochement did not coincide with British policy. Both the Foreign Office and the India Office considered Tibet's complete withdrawal from under Chinese influence absolutely out of the question.

A number of treaties had been concluded during the previous decade stipulating Tibet's inclusion in the sphere of this influence, and now the British government laid obstacles to changing the system created by it in central Asia on the strength of those treaties. It is quite natural that Dorjiev's activity was regarded as alien to the British interests. The Russian consul in Calcutta wrote: "Here they hate Dorjiev and fear the influence he has on the Dalai Lama."[14]

Meanwhile, Dorjiev went from Urga to St Petersburg. In the middle of February, he handed the "Memorandum on the Status of Tibet" to the foreign minister. This document had been drawn up after discussions with the Dalai Lama and his counsellors about the situation in Tibet and about her attitude towards China, Russia and Britain. After a series of such deliberations, the Dalai Lama had confirmed Dorjiev's powers, "thanks to which," the latter wrote, "I have been the only actual go-between in Tibet's contacts with Russia for 20 years already. I was provided with a letter and orders to conduct negotiations with the minister for foreign affairs for the purpose of learning whether Russia had completely abandoned all intercourse with Tibet."[15]

In his "Memorandum", the author summarized the events of the last years and linked them closely with events in Mongolia: "In 1907, China decided to destroy all traces of self-government in Tibet, having sent a detachment of well-armed troops with machine-guns under the command of Chao Erh-hsün for this purpose.[16] The forces began their actions in eastern Tibet in a distinctively Chinese way: they turned monasteries into ruins, desecrated sanctuaries, plundered precious objects, killed half the local population and caused the other half to scatter.

"The Chinese government, obviously greatly delighted with Chao Erh-hsün's activity and considering his task in Tibet fulfilled, transferred him to Mongolia and commissioned him to deal with the Mongolians with the same methods he had employed in Tibet. Luckily for the Mongolians, the Chinese revolution has radically called a halt to this enterprise. There is no doubt that if it were not for this, the Tibetan horrors would have been repeated in Mongolia. Due to its close proximity to the Russian borders, such actions would have compelled the Russian government, by force of circumstances, to armed intervention. During all this struggle, the English remained mute witnesses and did not help the Tibetans in any way." In Dorjiev's opinion, the moment was rather a favorable one for "the adjustment of relations between Russia and Tibet".[17]

Apart from this "Memorandum" handed to the foreign minister, Dorjiev delivered two letters from the Dalai Lama to the chairman of the council of ministers. In the letters, the adjustment of relations between the two parties was concretized with the request to recognize the political independence of Tibet.

The first letter gave consideration to cultural relations. Concerning Dorjiev, it said that he is "authorized to watch over the true faith. That is why we ask you to render him all gracious patronage." Here, the Dalai Lama also asked permission to have 15 lamas attached to the Buddhist temple in St Petersburg, "who will have the duty to offer prayers for Russia's prosperity for the duration of a hundred kalpas." (One kalpa equals 432 million years.) Another request was to admit specially commissioned young Tibetans to Russian educational institutions.

The Dalai Lama's other letter dealt mostly with politics. It informed the chairman that the noble and disinterested intercession on the part of Russia "was discussed by the supreme council of holy men, princes and dignitaries of Tibet, and it was decided to register it in the state annals and to establish inviolable, eternal accord and links between the Russian and Tibetan peoples."

Furthermore, the letter stated that, at the present occasion, Tibet "would like to declare, for general knowledge, the proclamation of our independence and about the election of us to be the sovereign supreme ruler of Tibet. England, however, opposes this, insisting upon Chinese suzerainty. Under these circumstances, we have grounds to be apprehensive about an intrusion into our border territory, not without England's leave, of Chinese, Bhutanese and Nepalese troops, against which we shall be unable to offer resistance. Thus China may interfere with our affairs again and destroy our independence, which has been achieved finally after such blood-filled events."

In this connection, the letter confirmed that Dorjiev had been authorized to conduct negotiations of enormous political significance, that is "on the establishment of friendship between Tibet and England with the assistance of Russia; on the recognition of our independence by both states; on the dispatch of diplomatic representatives of Russia and England to Lhasa—if it turns out that this is impossible due to the Anglo-Russian Agreement of 1907, maybe Russia and England will find it possible to enlist the cooperation of other great powers as well or alter the afore-mentioned agreement, which does not conform to the present situation, so that they might assure Tibet's inviolability; and on the accreditation of our representative, Tsannyid Khamchen Agvan Dorjiev.

"Remembering the most gracious patronage of Your Majesty, the Emperor," the letter concluded, "I hope for the settlement of the above-mentioned issues, for the everlasting friendship between Russia and Tibet."[18]

The reserve of the Russian party towards the Tibetan plans described in the letters made Lhasa undertake even further steps in the same direction. The new circumstances demanded forcing a reaction from Russia. Tibet needed international recognition, and Russia could take the first step on the way.

After two months, another letter from the Dalai Lama addressed to the Tsar was received in St Petersburg. The Tibetan leader pointed out that the relations between the Manchu dynasty and Tibet were purely of a religious character, namely, the relations of a religious devotee towards his lama-teacher. But since "the Chinese have displayed the obvious aspiration to seize Tibet in one way or another, the former relations are broken off completely and cannot be restored...Presently, reckoning on assistance from the great powers, Russia and England, the Tibetans have unanimously proclaimed their independence and have chosen us, the Dalai Lama, as the sovereign ruler of the entire country.

"Informing you of this, we ask the two great powers, Russia and England, to recognize our independence and to declare their recognition to other states.

"In view of the possibility of military and diplomatic measures against Tibet on the part of China, we ask both great powers, having discussed the issue jointly, to make China cease her claims and to render us help henceforth."

The letter also contained the request to attach a larger lot to the Buddhist temple being built in St Petersburg, as well as to provide His Majesty's patronage in every matter to the Senior Tsannyid Khamba, Agvan Dorjiev.[19]

The great powers were still the hope of the Tibetans, but the powers themselves had a different point of view. Distant Tibet did not sway their feelings and intentions, and they adhered sternly to the course of policy that had been worked out in the previous decades.

The Tibetans' request for recognition of their independence produced no reaction on the part of Russia. This was not the case on the part of Britain. But the result was quite contrary to what the Tibetans had expected, although it was nothing new for Britain. Since recognition of an independent Tibet would contradict the policy of Anglo-Chinese consent, measures were outlined in London to eliminate this burdensome independence.

Before long, the Tibetans had the opportunity to satisfy themselves that this was so. They, too, had no wish to remain passive and tried to come to an understanding with Great Britain through Russian mediation, in other words, to change her orientation from China to Russia in her Tibetan policy. These attempts were reasonable enough, since cordial consent between Russia, Britain and France—the Entente—was by this time not an unimportant factor in international life. Also Britain, in those days, was preoccupied mostly with the situation in Europe, not caring that much for Asia. This might make her waive Chinese friendship in favour of gaining some profit in Europe. And she might have waived it, but in fact she never did. There was no point in doing so, since the Tibetan motives did not touch Russia.

A true-to-life reflection of the circumstances was included in the Dalai Lama's next letter, dated August 18, 1913, and also addressed to the Tsar. In it, the Dalai Lama wrote that the Tibetan people "have the great desire to promulgate, so that it be generally known, the proclaimed independence of Tibet and our having been chosen as the supreme ruler of Tibet. But, taking into account that the English wish us to remain under Chinese rule, and in view of the serious apprehensions, based on the information at our disposal, of possible intrusion with England's leave of Chinese, Bhutanese and Nepalese troops into our border territory before we can prepare an armed resistance, which might give the Chinese a chance to interfere with our affairs and to bring to naught everything we have achieved by means of bloody strife—in view of all this, we commission the Tsannyid Khamchen, Agvan Dorjiev, to seek the advice and gracious decision of Your Majesty, the Emperor, on the following issues."

The first number on the list of issues was the request to assist in establishing friendly relations between Tibet and Great Britain through Russia's mediation. Next, the Dalai Lama requested the dispatch of diplomatic representatives of Russia and Britain to Lhasa and the grant of guarantees of Tibet's inviolability and neutrality. Also in this letter, for the first time in the short but intense correspondence between Russia and Tibet, the Dalai Lama asked for weapons for armed resistance to a Chinese onslaught that might come directly from China or via Nepal and Bhutan: "(We request) the sale of weapons and the dispatch of military instructors on a mission. And if buying arms in Russia will be considered inadmissible, we seek permission to transport them through her territory and by her roads." As before, the Dalai Lama reminded the Tsar of the necessity "to accredit our representative, Tsannyid Khamchen Agvan Dorjiev" and of his aspiration "to maintain friendly links between Russia and Tibet unshakeably forever, and to establish lively trading and economic ties between them by means of special contractual agreement."[20]

To execute the Dalai Lama's orders, Dorjiev presented the above-mentioned to the chairman of the Russian council of ministers. The chairman, Count V. N. Kokovtsov, however, passed this note over to Foreign Minister S. D. Sazonov to take a decision on the Tibetan inquiry, thus burying it safely since the ministry maintained its old position of complete aloofness towards Tibet. Russian weapons were not delivered.

The Dalai Lama thus strove for recognition of his supreme power in Tibet and of Tibet's independence from China. In this situation when, as the Tibetan ruler had put it, Britain was "opposing herself against it, insisting upon Chinese suzerainty", there remained, however, discrepancies between the British India government and Great Britain herself as to the methods for keeping Tibet under control. Colonial officials saw as the most effective way to maintain control the sending of an armed detachment to Lhasa, even if under the pretence of securing the Dalai Lama's safety. London did not share such a view.

As before, the discrepancy originated not from a lack of understanding of the British empire's goals by one of the parties, but simply from a disagreement about tactics. The colonial government in India was indeed a part of the empire's state machinery; but it was a part that was, to a certain extent, independent. Thus this government ventured to deviate from instructions from London about the measures to be taken with respect to Tibet.

For example, Younghusband, in his time, had considerably exceeded the limits of what London had permitted. Similar divergence displayed itself again when the police officer Laden-la was attached to the Dalai Lama on his departure from India, having accompanied the high priest in Darjeeling and Kalimpong. Previously, Laden-la had taken part in Younghusband's expedition. He knew both English and Tibetan, and professed Buddhism. The viceroy's administration hoped to plant him as its agent. It reckoned to have in the person of Laden-la some kind of equivalent to Dorjiev, who could serve the Dalai Lama as an intermediary with Britain in the way that the latter did with Russia.

But, while it was quite clear to the Dalai Lama that Dorjiev served the cause of Tibet faithfully, and that is why he asked the Russian government to recognize "the Tsannyid Khamchen" officially as a plenipotentiary of Tibet, he also knew it was impossible to count on Laden-la's services to Tibet. This is because there was no doubt about his loyal inclusion in a different service; and soon this inclusion was confirmed in a most unambiguous manner.

Laden-la's dispatch in the capacity of British representative attached to the Dalai Lama was negatively received in London. Despite the pretexts from India that it was too late to change anything, since "the representative" was already on Tibetan territory, the definite order to return him was given from Britain. Telegrams were sent to the British trade agent in Gyangtse, ordering him to detain Laden-la; but the latter, nevertheless, continued his travels. The explicit order to return caught up with him just 40 kilometers from Lhasa, and only this small distance separated the Indian government's plan from being realized. But again, he did not return from there so soon, because the viceroy's government did not insist on his immediately coming back although, even in the Dalai Lama's eyes, Laden-la was most probably a spy, and so there was no need to keep him in Tibet.

Since Tibet's independence contradicted the Chinese policy of the British empire, the London government sought to restore the formerly existent situation, in which it could impose Chinese suzerainty on Tibet without interfering in Tibetan affairs directly. This persuasion thus entailed a different tactic from that conceived by the British India government, and underlay Britain's plan to convene a conference on Tibetan issues.

On August 17, 1912 the British minister in Peking, Sir John Jordan, passed a memorandum of his government to the Chinese foreign ministry, the Wai-wu Pu. In this document, the British government pointed out the possibility of solving the problem of Tibet easily, not through military measures but by means of negotiation. It alluded to the recent talks between Jordan and Yüan Shih-k'ai, during which the Chinese armed expedition against Tibet had been mentioned.

The British government further set forth its views on ways of reaching this solution. According to the memorandum, Yüan Shih-k'ai's government was to abstain from any active interference in

Tibetan affairs, that is to say, by military means, and in general from sending Chinese troops there again. It expressed objection to the fact that Chinese officials had tried to concentrate Tibetan rule in their own hands during the past two years. Laying down these conditions, the memorandum actually warned Yüan Shih-k'ai against repetition of the mistakes made by the Ch'ing authorities.

The main condition of the settlement, according to the memorandum, was the acknowledgment of the suzerain rights of China in Tibet. This was supplemented with the recognition of the indisputable right of China to have her representative (i.e. the amban) in Lhasa with an appropriate escort.

The defeat of the Chinese military forces in Tibet made the government of Yüan Shih-k'ai try to restore, through political manoeuvres, the kind of Tibetan dependency that had existed during the rule of the Ch'ing authorities. Towards the end of October, 1912, Yüan Shih-k'ai promulgated a decree that read: "...the ex-Dalai Lama, being moved by a feeling of sincere devotion, wishes to restore links with China, All the slips and blunders he had committed in the past are to be forgiven, and he is to be reinstated in his high dignity, being given the honorary title "Ch'en-hsün Tsan-hua Hsi-tien Ta-shan Tse-tsai Fa" ("The Sincere, Submissive, Furthering Enlightenment, Great, Virtuous and Blissful Tibetan Reincarnate")." Granting the Dalai Lama a new title, Yüan Shih-k'ai's government acted in accordance with a tradition that had long since been formed in the Chinese empire. What was remarkable, in this case, was not just the very act of conferring the title, this act being similar to that performed by the Ch'ing authorities in 1908, but the absolute disregard of the real situation with its actual circumstances. The Dalai Lama did not need either a title or decree about his reinstatement.

The decree contained the words of the Dalai Lama that served as a ground for Yüan Shih-k'ai to issue it: "From the past winter up to the present moment, order in Tibet cannot be restored. In view of this, wishing to countenance the Buddhist religion, I ask to bring this to the notice of the president of the Republic, hoping that he will see that the appropriate measures are undertaken for it."[21] But there is not a hint of submission nor a wish to restore links in these words, no matter how they might be interpreted in the decree. The Dalai Lama spoke only about the necessity of recalling Chinese troops who were committing excesses in Tibet, and not about any reinstatement of himself.

In fact, most probably, there had never been any such address to the president on the part of the Dalai Lama. The words he had supposedly spoken are to be found only in this decree by Yüan Shih-k'ai. When and through whom they were to have been communicated is not known. But it is well known that the Dalai Lama never sought any opportunity to communicate with Yüan Shih-k'ai at the time.

Contemporary observers of Tibetan events have noted that Yüan Shih-k'ai's decree was totally unfounded. Russian diplomatic documents contain the appraisal, according to which this decree was "quite unexpected and difficult to understand. Judging by it, it appears that the Dalai Lama himself addressed the president to express his loyalty. Such a turn of events would have been completely contradictory to everything that had happened before."[22]

The Russian newspaper *Novoye Vremya* wrote at the same time, alluding to eyewitness information: "After their heroic year-and-a-half struggle the Tibetans, who fought almost with bare hands, have gained victory. Tens of thousands of Tibet's best sons have fallen in this unequal fight. All the more offensive for all of Tibet, then, seems the recent representation made by England in Peking—at their expense, but without their leave. Without any knowledge of the Dalai Lama and the Tibetan government, the English envoy has proposed to the government of China maintaining suzerainty over Tibet. It has rung all over the country as a disgraceful and outrageous insult."[23]

Yüan Shih-k'ai's decrees and telegrams about the Dalai Lama's reinstatement were aimed at disguising the concealed plans of his government which were, however, not long in becoming evident. As early as January, 1913, the newspaper *Beijing Ribao* wrote that "the temporary president of the Republic has proposed to the Committee on Mongolian and Tibetan Affairs that it draw up a draft of articles about Tibetan policy. The draft has been discussed by the council of ministers. It has been resolved not to consider Tibet a vassal domain, to sanction the right to govern her territory, to confer titles, to pay wages, to abolish the post of amban, and to establish a special administrative body."[24]

Although the Dalai Lama had every reason to take the abovementioned manoeuvres negatively, at the same time he could not ignore the aspiration of a certain faction of Tibetan monasteries and dignitaries to restore the Sino-Tibetan relations that had existed under the Ch'ing authorities and which had guaranteed a stable, elite position for them. As a sober politician, he had to take into account the possibility of a new Anglo-Chinese arrangement on Tibetan affairs, which might restore the former status of Tibet. His misgivings arose because of the previous Tibetan policy of the Powers. The proposed negotiations might give him the opportunity to try at least to dampen the war in eastern Tibet, even if by means of an agreement between the Tibetans and the Chinese.

The Anglo-Chinese negotiations in Peking led to the agreement about the necessity to hold a conference based on the memorandum of August 17. The question of the parties to the conference was finally settled: China, Britain and Tibet were to take part. The participation of the Tibetans was all the more necessary, because the Tibeto-Mongolian Treaty of 1913 restricted the arbitrariness of Tibet's opponents in the field of international rights. Thus, Britain approached the conference with an eye askew to the treaty.

The Chinese delegation to the conference was headed by Ch'en I-fan, appointed by presidential decree and filling the post of "Chief of the Tibetan Frontier District". He was assisted by Wang Hai-p'ing, holding the post of "Deputy Chief of the Tibetan Frontier District". These official ranks had been conferred on purpose. They were to show that the officials' membership in the conference was just a short-term errand from the president, and that their main task was to proceed to Lhasa and to gain a foothold there in their new positions.

At the head of the British delegation was Sir Arthur Henry McMahon. By the time of the conference he had been working in the political administration of British India for nearly a quarter of a century, and attained the position of state secretary in the viceroy's government in 1911. He had previously been preoccupied with the demarcation of the Afghan-Beluchi frontier and the investigation of the borders between India and Tibet. Frontier issues had became his "favorite" field. He saw as his main task at the conference the establishment of a frontier line such as would clearly separate unquiet Tibet from the Indian estates. Later, this line gained the name of "the McMahon Line", and nowadays is known as the `hotline' of the border between India and the People's Republic of China.

During the preparation period for the conference, British Foreign Minister Grey asserted to his Russian counterpart, Sazonov, via the Russian ambassador to London, Benckendorff, that the government of Russia would be kept fully informed about the progress of negotiations. However, these assertions remained mere words.

The viceroy's government ignored Russian consul general Nabokov throughout the conference. It did not even agree to such a trifling point as the consul's presence in Simla, venue of the conference.

Nabokov reported to St Petersburg in this connection: "Under the present conditions of openly and distinctly displayed unwillingness of the viceroy's government to keep me informed about the course of negotiations, my further stay in Simla might only be interpreted in the sense of my aspiration to obtain the tidings in a roundabout fashion. I dare say that, staying here, I would have thus been simply deviating needlessly from the position I have adopted from the very beginning, the dignity of this position being incompatible with any `roundabout ways'."[25]

Further reports from India to the Russian foreign ministry bore the signs of obvious annoyance at the reticence of British colleagues, whose only answer to the most harmless questions was, "I don't know." Resenting them, Nabokov left Simla. Only the concluding documents of the conference were subsequently sent by diplomatic channels. But this lack of information about the course of the conference and the consequent impossibility to alter its results did not perturb the Russian foreign ministry.

To make the impression complete, let us quote the British author who elaborated upon the theme in detail and summed up the opinion of the highest-ranking British diplomatic officers in London: "Sazonov was really implying that `It does not matter what we (British) do in Tibet, if only it is done sub rosa'."[26] This dictum may serve as a final chord to the entire Tibetan policy of Russia.

While Ch'en I-fan was dragging out the acceptance of decisions on the issues discussed, hoping for a change in the situation more favorable for his government, and hence for more beneficial results of the conference, an Anglo-Tibetan agreement on the border between British India and Tibet was achieved. On May 24 and 25, the British and Tibetan plenipotentiaries exchanged notes fixing the adoption of the McMahon Line as the border between India and Tibet. In his note to McMahon, Lönchen Shatra informed him that the map of the border had been considered by the Tibetan government in Lhasa, which gave the instruction to adopt the border as it was marked on the map by the red line.

The war growing imminent in Europe deprived the British government of any opportunity to be engaged in matters other than European ones. The Simla Conference was curtailed brusquely. Nevertheless, McMahon, together with Lönchen Shatra, signed the

Anglo-Tibetan Declaration about shouldering the obligations contained in the Simla Convention that had been discussed at the conference and initialled by the three parties. The Anglo-Tibetan Trade Regulations were also signed. This was contrary to instructions from London, though nominally the interdiction of signing separate agreements without China was not violated.

A month after the conclusion of the Simla Conference, Britain had declared herself in a state of war against Germany: World War I had begun. By this time, the main author of the Simla documents, Sir Henry McMahon, had already left the shores of India, never to return. He was appointed British high commissioner in Egypt. Ch'en I-fan never reached Tibet, either in the rank of "tzu-an fu-shih" or in any other capacity. Lönchen Shatra reported to his government on his return to Lhasa that he considered the convention to be a guarantee against Chinese intrusion, and that the convention was now open for Chinese signature.

The Peking government never signed the Anglo-Tibetan Declaration, and the Simla Convention has remained incomplete in the sense of lacking its final ratification. Nonetheless, this does not reduce its significance as an international document reflecting the essence of the parties' relations that resulted from the development of events in Tibet and around it. Agvan Dorjiev and Lord Curzon were at the origin of this development.

Marcus Aurelius, emperor of Ancient Rome and Stoic philosopher, once declared that a man is worth what his goal is worth. Dorjiev's goal—a free and independent Tibet—was attained, though not quite in the way he followed; and he himself, as a diplomat and the Dalai Lama's representative, fixed this achievement in a document of international law—namely, the Tibeto-Mongolian Treaty of 1913. Curzon, on the other hand, aspired to increase and extend the power and the grandeur of the British empire. But the latter did not accept his services, having a different notion of her interests.

In the course of the decades that have passed since then, the world community has endured wars, cruelties and bloodshed to the denial of imperial ambition and interests, regardless of their origin. It has also come to acknowledge the priority of freedom and independence. Looking back, a retrospective view on the collision between Dorjiev and Curzon, who conducted and embodied certain state policies of their countries, allows us to determine with certainty who was who in this struggle.

Conclusion

The concluding remarks of this book are intended to show the immediate bond between the past and the present—between the Simla Conference and the McMahon Line on one hand, and the present Sino-Indian border/territorial dispute on the other. Almost 80 years ago Tibet, as an independent participant of this conference, recognized the McMahon Line as the legal frontier with India. More recently, in 1959, a defenceless Tibet represented by her exiled leadership addressed the following argument to the government of India: if you consider the McMahon Line to be the legal border between the two states, then you should recognize as well the demand for Tibet's independence as being legal.

This argument in favour of an independent Tibet can hardly be considered sufficient and comprehensive. But it does play a certain part in the chain of other arguments. What is important and deserves the highest appraisal is the broad and active campaign of international public organizations for protection of the rights of Tibet to self-determination and her own form of government.

Let us give one more reason in favour of the true self-determination of all peoples. Similar to the former USSR, the problem of nationalities was solved in China not on the basis of free expression of the people's will, but by means of force. Historical experience has shown that in the former Soviet Union, the forcible settlement of the nationalities problem finally led to growing hostility between peoples, human losses and the split-up of the state.

Tibet has no less rich a history of her own form of government than the former Soviet republics. Proof of this are the military and diplomatic events at the beginning of the 20th century that led to the total break between Tibet and China lasting until the middle of the century. The many centuries old, friendly proximity of the two nations was gone in a moment, replaced by hostility and military confrontation. The realistic appraisal of all these factors and the drawing of appropriate conclusions should result in processes that will be the logical continuation of the past into the present.

The return of the Dalai Lama to Tibet that was planned a few years ago might have become the most important of these processes. However, this would only have happened provided the Tibetans were satisfied with their status in their country and lived there happily. The stern reality presents an altogether different picture.

Now, the prospects of settling the problems of the Tibetan people are seen in terms of the joint efforts of the world community, with the Peoples' Republic of China taking part. Hopefully, such efforts will finally result in satisfying the legal requirements of the time and allowing Tibet to take her rightful place among the free nations of the world.

NOTES

Introduction

1. Since this book was written, John Snelling has published his book on Dorjiev entitled *Buddhism in Russia: the Story of Agvan Dorzhiev, Lhasa's Emissary to the Tsar*. His work was welcomed in my book review in *Asian Affairs*, London, June 1995.
2. Lamb, A., *Britain and Chinese Central Asia*, London 1960, p.262.
3. Grunfeld, T., *The Making of Modern Tibet*, London 1987, pp.49-59.
4. Marshall, Julie G. *Britain, China and Tibet 1765-1947. The Background to the India-China Border Dispute. A Select Bibliography*, Bundoora: La Trobe University, 1977.
5. MacGregor, J., *Tibet. A Chronicle of Exploration*, London 1970, p.283.
6. Other prominent figures accused of being Russian 'agents' include Madame Blavatsky the Theosophist, who also played an important role in the early development of the Indian National Congress; and Nikolai Roerich, the painter and philosopher who travelled widely in India and Central Asia in the 1920s.
7. Curzon continued to be preoccupied with the potential threat from Russia long after his return from India. After the First World War, he served as Foreign Secretary and in that capacity campaigned against Bolshevik subversion in Afghanistan and Persia.
8. *Zhongguo jindai shigao*, Beijing 1984, p.269.
9. Zhou Weizhou, *Yinge qinlue Xizang shilue*, Xian 1984, p.109.
10. Waddell, L.A., *Lhasa and its Mysteries*, London 1929, p.53.
11. Lamb, A., *The McMahon Line*, London 1966, pp.75-76.
12. Shakabpa, W.D., *Tibet. A political history*, Yale 1967, p.116.

Chapter One

1. Fairbank, J.K. *Trade and Diplomacy on the China Coast*, Cambridge, Mass. 1953, p.462.
2. Liu Guan'i, *Diguozhuyi qinlue Xizang dianshi*, Beijing 1951, p.8; Huang Fensheng, *Xizang qingkuang*, Shanghai 1954, p.110.
3. The only people with access to these archives have been Chinese historians preparing their official histories of the reigns of

certain governors or emperors. The period preceding the downfall of the Ch'ing dynasty is described in the 530th volume of *Ch'ing-shih Kao* (*Chronicle of Ch'ing History*), which was published in Peking at the end of the 1920s. These volumes were prepared according to a scheme perfected centuries ago: everything in them had to testify to the wisdom of the ruler under discussion. Even the *Chi'ing-shih Kao* volume contains nothing critical of the Ch'ing dynasty, although this had already been overthrown at the time it was written.

4. Russian Foreign Policy Archive (RFPA), f.1448, p.2.
5. Ibid, f.1448, p.32.
6. Ibid., f.1448, p.162.
7. Ibid, f.1440, pp.162-163.
8. Ibid, f.1448, p.164.
9. Ibid, f.1448, p.163.
10. Ibid, f.1448, p.164.
11. Landon, P., *Lhasa*, London 1905, p.6.
12. The names are given as transliterated from the Russian archives. The spelling is not exact as the Tibetan language was unfamiliar to the Russian ear, and there was no written version.
13. RFPA, f.1462, p.3. It might at first seem strange that the Tibetans considered approaching Britain, since they feared a British invasion. However, as will be seen, the policies of British officials in London often differed from the views of their colleagues in India.
14. Ibid, f.1450, p.21.
15 .Ibid, f.1450, p.21.
16. Ibid., f.1448, p.11.
17. Tsar Nicholas II had travelled to the Far East while he was still a prince legate. However, a Samurai fanatic made an attempt on his life while he was in Japan: this incident cast a cloud over his journey, which did not result in any changes in the direction of Russian foreign policy.
18. RFPA, f.1448, p.98. Here, as in many other cases, the phrase 'hostile Englishmen' is a reference not to England itself but rather to Lord Curzon's administration in British India.
19. *Times*, June 26, 1901.
20. *Odesskiye Novosti*, June 15, 1901.
21. Kolmaš, J., *Tibet and Imperial China*, Canberra 1967, p.57.

Chapter Two

1. Russian Foreign Policy Archive (RFPA), f.1450, p.37.
2. Lattimore, Owen, *Inner Asian Frontiers of China*, New York 1940, p.236.
3. RFPA, Diplomatic Archive, Government of India, No. 87, p.36.
4. RFPA, Dip. Arch., Nos. 74-79, p.19.
5. RFPA, f.1448, p.178.
6. RFPA, Dip. Arch., No. 78, in. No. 130-170, p.26.
7. RFPA, f.1450, p.37.
8. Ibid., No. 30, ind. No. 484-503, p.21.
9. Ibid., No. 80, 81, 84-87, p.69.
10. Ibid., Nos. 80, 81, 84-87, p.65.
11. RFPA, Dip. Arch., National Archives of India, Foreign Secret, Nos. 1-88.
12. Mehra, P., *The Younghusband Expedition*, Asia Publishing House 1969.
13. *Zhongguo jindai shigao*, Beijing 1984, p.30.
14. Cited in *The Younghusband Expedition* by P. Mehra, London 1968, p.200.
15. RFPA, f.1449, p.118.

Chapter Three

1. For a new biography of Younghusband see: French, P., *Younghusband: the Last Great Imperial Adventurer*, London 1994.
2. Russian Foreign Policy Archive (RFPA), f.1451, p.67.
3. Ibid., f.1451, p.67.
4. Mehra, P., op. cit,, pp.180-190-193.
5. *Times of Ceylon*, November 18, 1903.
6. Lamb, A., *Britain and Chinese Central Asia*, London 1960, p.293.
7. RFPA, f.1451, p.38.
8. Ibid., f.1450, pp.131-132.
9. Candler, E. *The Unveiling of Lhasa*, London 1905, pp.102, 109.
10. RFPA, Diplomatic Archive, No. 140, p.161.
11. Waddell wrote that there was much evidence to prove that Russian rifles and ammunition had been delivered to Lhasa. In the Darjeeling bazaar there were rumors, confirmed by a Japanese monk returning from Lhasa in 1903, that 200 camels loaded with rifles had been received from the Russian government. The absurdity of this information is especially obvious against the background of Younghusband's report.

Chapter Four

1. Li Tieh-tseng, *Tibet. Today and Yesterday*, New York 1960, p.93.
2. Landon, P., *op. cit.*, p.304.
3. Russian Foreign Policy Archive (RFPA), f.1456, pp.71-72.
4. *The Times*, March 3, 1910.
5. Chapman, Francis Spencer, *Lhasa: the Holy City*, London 1940, p.137.
6. RFPA, f.1453, p.140.
7. Lamb, A., *Britain and Chinese Central Asia*, London 1960, p.316.
8. RFPA, f.1466, p.15-17, 21.
9. Ibid., f.1466, p.58.
10. Ostrikov, P.I., *Imperialisticheskaya politica Anglii v. Kitae, 1900-1914*, Moscow 1978, pp.195-197.
11. Ibid., f.1451, p.67.
12. Ibid., f.1451, p.67.
13. The Dalai Lama was almost the only significant political leader who objected to the convention. He declared more than once that he would not recognize any Tibetan agreements with England which he had not signed personally (see RFPA, f.1456, p.169.)
14. In July, 1904 the futility of these searches became known. The Russian embassy in London informed St Petersburg: "The impression is common here that England has been mistaken in its estimation of the commercial prospects of Tibet," (see RFPA, f.1451, p.43).
15. Russia would have been unable to acquire Tibet for purely geographical reasons since the two countries had no common border: in the south Tibet bordered on British India, Nepal and Bhutan and was surrounded on all other sides by China.
16. RFPA, f.1452, p.20.
17. Ibid., f.1484, p.8.

Chapter Five

1. Russian Foreign Policy Archive (RFPA), f.1466, p.5.
2. Ibid., f.1466, p.5.
3. Ibid., f.1455, p.95.
4. *Ch'ing-shih Kao*, Vol. 530 (place of publication not shown), 1927, p.23.
5. RFPA, f.1456, p.3.
6. Ibid., f.1455, p.5.

7. Ibid., f.1455, p.74.
8. Ibid., f.1451, p.91.
9. Ibid., f.1455, p.102.
10. Ibid., f.1455, p.80, 49.
11. Ibid., f.1455, p.128.
12. Lamb, A., *The McMahon Line*, London 1966, p.9.
13. RFPA, f.1455, p.61.
14. Ibid., f.1455, p.38.
15. Ibid., f.1454, pp.80-82.
16. Lamb, A., *The McMahon Line*, p.10.
17. RFPA, f.1464, p.2.
18. Ibid., f.1452, p.19.
19. Ibid., f.1464, p.17, 34.
20. Ibid., f.1468, p.16.
21. Xin-hai Revolution of 1911 to 1913: collection of documents and materials, Moscow, 1968, pp.38-40.
22. RFPA, f.1464, p.36.
23. Ibid, f.1454, p.52.
24. Ibid, f.1454, p.12.
25. Ibid, f.1468, p.8.

Chapter Six

1. Russian Foreign Policy Archive (RFPA), f.1451, p.88.
2. Landon, P., op. cit., p.398.
3. Christie, C., "Great Britain, China and Tibet, 1911-1921", *Modern Asian Studies*, Oct., 1976, vol. 10, part 4.
4. She Su, op. cit., p.135.
5. Mehra, P.L., *The Younghusband Expedition*, p.352.
6. MacGregor, J., op. cit., p.323.
7. Despite the hesitations of the London government and the head of the empire himself concerning the appraisal of Younghusband's mission, his services and those of the majority of the officers who took part in the expedition finally did receive official recognition. Although in general they received awards and advancement, nevertheless the award list did not promote Younghusband to the rank of colonel but left him a major, as he had been before the expedition.
8. This office was situated in Peking. Functioning in close connection with the Tsung-li Ya-men, it served as a permanent channel of foreign influence, mainly British, upon the Ch'ing government.

9. RFPA, f.1458, p.27.
10. Ibid., f.1456, p.169.
11. MacGregor, J., op. cit., p.351.
12. Ibid., p.286.
13. Ukhtomskiy, E.E., *Iz oblasti lamaizma: Kokhodu anglichang na Tibet*, St Petersburg, 1904, p.3.
14. Lamb, A., *The McMahon Line*, p.189.

Chapter Seven

1. Russian Foreign Policy Archive (RFPA), f.1452, p.946.
2. Ibid., p.123.
3. Ibid., p.145.
4. Ibid., p.150.
5. Ibid., p.145.
6. Ibid., p.227-228.
7. Ibid., f.1468, p.9.
8. Lamb, A., *The McMahon Line*, p.110.
9. Ibid., p.87.
10. Ibid., p.255.
11. Ibid., p.89.
12. Ibid., p.255.
13. RFPA, f.1452, p.214.
14. Ibid.
15. Ibid., p.226.
16. Ibid., p.28.
17. Ostaltseva, A.F., *Anglo-Russkaya Conventsia 1907* (British-Russian Convention), Saratov 1978, p.146.

Chapter Eight

1. Russian Foreign Policy Archive (RFPA), f.1475, p.4.
2. Ibid., f.1471, p.5.
3. Ibid., f.1458, p.14.
4. Ibid., p.29.
5. *Sankt-Peterburgskie Vedomosti*, April 7, 1910.
6. RFPA, f.1458, p.110.
7. Woodman D., *Himalayan Frontiers*, London 1969, p.142.

Chapter Nine

1. Russian Foreign Policy Archive (RFPA), f.1452, p.75.
2. Ibid., p.2.

3. Ibid., f.1452, p.48.
4. Ibid., f.1464, p.92.
5. Ibid., f.1455, p.110.
6. Ibid., p.96.
7. According to one of Pokotilov's reports, "The Dalai Lama cherishes the most definite plans concerning the political union between Mongolia and Tibet. Having united, both countries should achieve liberation from Chinese supremacy. The Dalai Lama considered it to be necessary to organize active propaganda in this respect." Cf. Ibid., f.1463, p.25. The Russian consul to Urga expressed the same idea in his letter: "The Dalai Lama would not give up thoughts about the political alliance of Tibet and Mongolia on religious grounds and under his personal guidance." Cf. Ibid., f.1646, p.50. In time, these plans became firmly established. It became known from Mongolian sources that "the Dalai Lama with his confederates, the Mongolian princes and influential khutughtu-gegens, have, in principle, irrevocably decided to separate from China and form an independent union, having realized this action under the patronage of and with support from Russia, thus avoiding bloodshed." Cf. Ibid., f.1157, p.33.
8. Ibid., p.34.
9. Ibid., f.1463, p.33.
10. Ibid., f.1456, p.136.
11. Ibid., f.1455, p.34.
12. Ibid., f.1464, p.102.
13. Ibid., f.1456, p 108.
14. Ibid., f.1464, p 79.
15. Ibid., f.1456, p.75.
16. Ibid., f.1465, p.60.
17. Ibid., f.1452, p.44.
18. Ibid., f.1465, p.60.
19. Ibid., f.1456, p.173.
20. Ibid., f.1457, p.61.
21. Ibid., f.1468, p.44.
22. Ibid., f.1457, p.107.
23. Ibid., f.1462, p.2.
24. Ibid., p.27.
25. Ibid., p.55.
26. Ibid., p.53.
27. Ibid., f.1455, p.41.

28. Ibid., p.29.
29. Hundreds of these pilgrims at times came to Lhasa to see the Dalai Lama. Consul Lyuba reported that "Buryats and Kalmyks of Astrakhan are freely gathering in Urga. I suppose there are no grounds to lay obstacles for Kalmyks from the Don River who wish to come here." Cf. Ibid., f.1467, p.4.
30. Ibid., f.1455, p.33.
31. Ibid., p.144.
32. Ibid., p.148.
33. Ibid., f.1457, p.23.
34. Ibid., p.24.
35. Ibid., p.33.
36. Ibid., p.44.
37. The Anglo-Chinese Convention of 1890.
38. RFPA, f.1456, p.32.
39. Ibid., f.1457, p.52.
40. Ibid., f.1457, p.55.
41. Ibid., f.1456, p.172.
42. Ibid., p.197.
43. Ibid., p.108.
44. Ibid., p.131.
45. Ibid., p.135.
46. Ibid., f.1468, p.16-17.
47. Ibid., p.19-20.
48. Ibid., f.1468, pp.19-20.
49. Ibid., f.1456, p.84.
50. Ibid., f.1472, p.59.
51. Ibid., p.59.
52. Ibid., p.60.
53. Ibid., f.1456, p.59.
54. In the emperor's edict issued on this occasion, it was written: "In accordance with ancient laws, the Dalai Lama has previously already received the title of Hsi-t'ian Ta-shan Ts'u-tsai Fu ("The Outstanding Self-born Buddha of the Western Heavens"). Henceforth, this title is supplemented with Cheng-shun Ts'ang-hua...("The Sincerely Devoted...", after which the same title is to be repeated)." Cf. *Ch'ing-shih Kao*, p.23.
55. Teichman E., *Travels of a Consular Official in Eastern Tibet*, Cambridge 1922, p.15.
56. *Buddhism and State in the Far East* (*Buddhism i Cosudarstvo na Dalnjem Vostoke*), Moscow 1987, p.49.

57. RFPA f.1466, p.42.
58. Willoughby, M. E., "Report on the Work of the Mission Engaged on the Repatriation of the Chinese Garrison of Lhasa, Which Surrendered to the Tibetans in August 1912." Simla 1912, p.118.

Chapter Ten

1. Russian Foreign Policy Archive (RFPA), f.1458, p.52.
2. Ibid., Diplomatic Archive, Government of India, No. 38, ind. No. 305-510, doc. 454.
3. RFPA, f.1458, p.58.
4. Ibid., p.26.
5. Ibid., p.147.
6. Ibid., f.1458, p.147.
7. Ibid., p.145.
8. Ibid., f.1480, p.69.
9. Ibid., f.1458, p.74.
10. Ibid., f.1458, p.74.
11. Ibid., p.75.
12. *Rossiya*, May 13, 1910.
13. RFPA, f.1458, p.59.
14. Ibid., f.1458, p.59.
15. Ibid., p.111.
16. Ibid., f.1480, p.107.
17. Ibid., f.1468, p.19.
18. Ibid., f.1458, p.155.
19. Ibid., f.1457, p.221.
20. Ibid., p.223.
21. Ibid., p.225.
22. Ibid., p.226.
23. Ibid., p.229.
24. Ibid., f.1458, p.252.
25. Ibid., p.253.
26. Ibid., p.290.
27. Ibid., f.1480, p.16.
28. Ibid., f.1457, p.33.
29. Ibid., f.1458, p.290.
30. Ibid., p.299.
31. Ibid., f.1458, p.302.
32. Lamb, A., *The McMahon Line*, p.414.
33. RFPA, f.1458, p.303.
34. Ibid., p.110.

35. Se Pin, *Gofang yu waitsiao* (*Defence of the State and Foreign Relations*), Shanghai 1932, p.43.
36. RFPA, f.1480, p.56.
37. Ibid., p.68.
38. Hua Ts'e-yu, *Chung-kuo Pien-tsang (The Frontiers of China)*, Shanghai 1932, p.303.
39. Fang Se-min, *Hsi-tsang (Tibet)*, Shanghai 1954, p.26.

Chapter Eleven

1. *Rech*, April 1, 1911.
2. Russian Foreign Policy Archive (RFPA), f.1458, p.174.
3. Ibid., f.1456, p.247.
4. Ibid., f.1458, p.337.
5. Ibid, f.1476, p.15.
6. Ibid, f.1458, p.332.
7. Ibid., p.276.
8. Ibid., f.1458, p.278.
9. Ibid., f.1476, p.24.
10. Ibid., f.412 (248), p.81-84.
11. Ibid., p.90-91.
12. Bell, Sir C., *Tibet, Past & Present*, Oxford 1924, p.151.
13. RFPA, f.1476, p.41-43.
14. Ibid., p.56.
15. Ibid., p.68.
16. Dorjiev probably did not know that troops in Tibet were directly headed by Chao Erh-feng, his brother.
17. RFPA, f.1476, p.68.
18. Ibid., f.1476, p.95.
19. Ibid., f.1466, p.99-100.
20. Ibid., p.96.
21. Ibid., f.412 (248), p.44.
22. Ibid., f.412 (248), p.44.
23. *Novoye Vremiya*, February 16, 1913.
24. *Beijing Ribao*, January 18, 1913.
25. RFPA, f.1476, p.116.
26. Woodman D., *Himalayan Frontiers*, London 1969, p.151.

Bibliography

A. Primary Sources: Archival materials

Russian language

Russian Foreign Policy Archives (RFPA), Ministry of Foreign Affairs of Russia, Chinese section 80k:
RFPA, f.412 (248). RFPA, f.1448. RFPA, f.1450. RFPA, f.1451. RFPA, f.1452. RFPA, f.1453. RFPA, f.1454. RFPA, f.1455. RFPA, f.1456. RFPA, f.1457. RFPA, f.1458. RFPA, f.1463. RFPA, f.1464. RFPA, f.1465. RFPA, f.1466. RFPA, f.1467. RFPA, f.1468. RFPA, f.1471. RFPA, f.1475. RFPA, f.1476. RFPA, f.1480. RFPA, f.1481.
RFPA, Middle Asia section, f.915.
RFPA, St. Petersburg, Main Arch., list 8, f:2.
Central State Military-History Archives, f.BYA.

*English language**

RFPA, Diplomatic Archives, Government of India, Foreign Department (Government of India [GoI]): GoI, no.5, indiv.no.315-409. GoI, no.6, indiv.no.70-386. GoI, no.10, indiv.no.170-509. GoI, no.30, indiv. no.484-503. GoI, no.38, indiv. no.385-510. GoI, no.75, indiv. no.78-108. GoI, no.78, indiv. no.130-172. GoI, no.74-79. GoI, nos.80, 81, 82, 84, 85, 86, 87.
(* Film-copies of documents in National Archives of India, Delhi.)
GoI, no.140. GoI, indiv.no.256. GoI, 578-726.

B. Published Documents

Russian language

K voprosu o kitaysko-indiyskoi granitse (On the Problem of the Chinese-Indian Border). Peking, 1962.
Russko-kitayskie otnoshenia (Russian-Chinese Relations), 1689-1916, Ofitsialnye dokumenty (Official Documents). Moscow, 1958.

Chinese language

Da Qin Li chao shi lu (Chronicle of the Rule of the Great Dynasty Qin). Tokyo, 1937.
Qin Shih Kao (Materials on Qin History). Place of publication not given, 1923, ts.530.

C. Literature

Russian Language

B-n L., *Khambo-Agvan Dorjiev, K borbie Tibeta za nezavisimost* (B-n, L., Khambo-Agvan Dorjiev, on the Struggle of Tibet for Freedom). New East, Moscow, 1923, vol.3.
Bogoslovsky V., Moskalev A., *Tibetskiy autonomy rayon KNR* (Tibet Autonomous Region of China). Moscow, 1978.
Chou Enlai, *Isbrannyie proisvedenia* (Selected Works). Peking, 1981.
Grimm E.M., *Sbornik dogovorov i drugih dokumentov po istorii mezdunarodnyh otnoshenii na Dalniem Vostoke, 1842-1925* (Collection of Agreements on the History of International Relations in the Far East). Moscow, 1927.
Grulev M.V., *Sopernichestvo Rossii i Anglii v Sredhei Asii* (Rivalry of Russia and England in Middle Asia). St. Petersburg, 1909.
Hedin Sven, *V serdtse Asii* (In the Heart of Asia). St. Petersburg, 1899.
Ignatiev A.V., *Vneshnia politika Rossii v 1905-1907* (Foreign Policy of Russia, 1905-1907). Moscow, 1966.
Khalfin N.A., *Lord Kerzon—ideolog i politik britanskogo imperialisma* (Lord Curzon, Ideologist and Politician of British Imperialism). Novaia i noveishaia istoria, no.I, 1983.
Khvostov V.M., *Istoria Diplomatii* (History of Diplomacy). Moscow, 1963.
Kitai i sosedi (China and its Neighbors). Moscow, 1982.
Koslov P.K., *Tibet i Dalai Lama* (Tibet and the Dalai Lama). Petersburg, 1920.
Kuleshov N.S., *Kitai i prigimalaiskie strany* (China and Himalayan Countries). Moscow, 1982.
Lamaism v Buriatii XVIII i nachala XX (Lamaism in Buriatia in the 18th and the early 20th centuries). Novosibirsk, 1983.
Leontiev V.P., *Inostrannaia ekspansia v Tibete* (Foreign Intervention in Tibet). Moscow, 1956.

Martynov M.S., *Status Tibeta v XVII-XVIII vekah* (Status of Tibet in the 17th and 18th centuries). Moscow, 1978.
Novaia istoria Kitaia (New History of China). Moscow, 1972.
Ostaltseva A.F., *Anglo-russkaia konventsia 1907* (Anglo-Russian Convention of 1907). Saratov, 1978.
Ostrikov P.I., *Imperialisticheskaia politika Anglii v Kitae, 1900-1914* (Imperialistic Policy of England in China). Moscow, 1978.
Popov A., *Rossia i Tibet* (Russia and Tibet). Novyi Vostok, 1927, vol.3.
Ruir, *Anglo-russokoie sopernichestvo v Asii v XIX veke* (Anglo-Russian Rivalry). Moscow, 1924.
Sinhaiskaia revoliutsia 1911-1913. Sbornik dokumentov i materialov (Xinhai Revolution. Collection of Documents and Materials). Moscow, 1968.
Tikhvinski S.L., *O sootnoshenii natsionalnogo i sotsialnogo voprosov v Sinhaiskoi revoliutsii* (On Correspondence of National and Social Problems in the Xinhai Revolution). Moscow, 1980.
Uhktomski E.E., *Is oblasti lamaisma* (On the Sphere of Lamaism). St Petersburg, 1904.
Vzaimootnoshenia Rossly so stranamy Vostoka v seredine XIX-nachale XX veka (Russian Relations with Countries of the East). Irkutsk, 1982.
Zapiska generala M.D.Skobeleva o pohode v Indiyu. Voennaia Encyclopedia, t.X (Note of General Skobelev on Conquest of India. Military Encyclopedia, vol.X). St. Petersburg, 1912.

Chinese Language

Bai Meiju, *Xizang Shimo ji yao* (The Greatest Knowledge on Tibet). Peking, 1931.
Chang Chungfu, *Zhonghua mingo waijiao shi* (History of the International Relations of the Chinese Republic). Chungqing, 1943.
Chou Weichou, *YingE qinlue wogo Xizang shilue* (Story of the Aggression of England and Russia against our Tibet). Shensi, 1984.
Fang Sinmin, *Xizang* (Tibet). Shanghai, 1954.
Gao Chagzhu, *Bianjiang u gofang* (Borders and Defence). Taibei, 1961.
Hu Sheng, *Diguo zhuyi u Zhonggo zhengzhi* (Imperialism and Policy of China), 1840-1927. Peking, 1978.
Hua Tsiu, *Zhonggo bianjiang* (Chinese Borders). Shanghai, 1932.
Huang Fengshen, *Xizang qingkuang* (The Situation in Tibet). Shanghai, 1954.

Se Bin, *Gofang u waijiao* (Defence of State and Foreign Connections). Shanghai, 1932.
Se Bin, *Xizang jiaoshe lue shi* (A Short History of Tibetan Negotiation). Shanghai, 1931.
She Su, *Qinggji Yingguo qinlue Xizang shi* (History of the Aggression of England in Tibet in Qin period). Peking, 1959.
Wu Siangsiang, *Edi qinlue zhonggo shi* (History of Aggression of Russian Imperialism in China). Taibei, 1973.
Ying Mei, *diguozhuyi qinlue Xizang shi liao* (History of Anglo-American Aggression in Tibet). Place of publication not indicated, 1950.
Zhonggo jindai shi (History of China in the New Period). Peking, 1931.
Zhonggo jindai shigao (New History of China). Peking, 1984.
Shahuan Egode qinlue Kuozhang (Development of Aggression of the Tsar's Russia). Peking, 1978.

English Language

Ahmad Z., *China and Tibet*, 1708-1958. Oxford, 1960.
Addy P., *Tibet on the Imperial Chessboard*. Calcutta, 1984.
Bell C., *Tibet, Past and Present*. Oxford, 1924.
Candler S., *The Unveiling of Lhasa*. London, 1905.
Chapman F., *Lhasa: the Holy City*. New York, 1972.
Chowdhury J.N., "British Contribution to the Confusion of Tibet's Status". *Quest*, Bombay, no.54, 1967.
Christie C., "Great Britain, China and Tibet, 1914-1921". *Modern Asian Studies*, Vol.10, part 4. London, 1976.
Curzon G.N., *Russia in Central Asia in 1889*. London, 1967.
Epstein I., *Tibet Transformed*. Peking, 1983.
Fairbank J.K., *China's Foreign Policy in Historical Perspective*. New York, 1969.
Fairbank J.K., *Synarchy under the Treaties*. Chicago, 1957.
Ghosh S., *Tibet in Sino-Indian Relations, 1899-1914*. Delhi, 1977.
Huttenback R., "The 'Great Game' in the Pamirs". *Modern Asian Studies*, vol.9. London, February 1975.
Kawaguchi E., *Three years in Tibet*. London, 1909.
Kolmash J., "Ch'ing shih kao on Modern History of Tibet". *Archiv Orientalni*. Prague, 1964, no.32.
Kolmash J., *Tibet and Imperial China*. Canberra, 1967.
Lamb A., *Britain and Chinese Central Asia, 1767-1907*. London, 1960.

Lamb A., *The McMahon Line*. London, 1966.
Landon P., *Lhasa*. London, 1905.
Lattimore O., *Inner Asia Frontiers of China*. New York, 1940.
MacGregor J., *Tibet: A Chronicle of Exploration*. London, 1970.
Marshall J., *Britain and Tibet, 1765-1947*. Bundoora, 1977.
Maxwell N., *India's China War*. London, 1970.
Mehra P., *McMahon Line and After*. Delhi, 1974.
Mehra P.L., *Tibetan Polity, 1904-37*. Wiesbaden, 1976.
Mehra P.L., *The Younghusband Expedition: an Interpretation*. Asian Publishing House, 1967.
Shakabpa W.D., *Tibet: A Political History*. Yale University, 1967.
Teichman E., *Travels of a Consular Official in Eastern Tibet*. Cambridge, 1922.
Tieh-tseng Li, *Tibet, Today and Yesterday*. New York, 1960.
Tsung Lien Shen, Shen Chi Lin, *Tibet and the Tibetans*. New York, 1973.
Waddel L., *Lhasa and its Mysteries*. London, 1929.
Willoughby M.E., *Report on the Work of the Mission Engaged on the Repatriation of the Chinese Garrison of Lhasa which Surrendered to the Tibetans in August 1912*. Simla, 1912.
Wright S., *Hart and the Chinese Customs*. Belfast, 1950.
Woodman D., *Himalayan Frontiers: A Political Review of British, Chinese, Indian and Russian Rivalries*. London, 1969.

D. Periodical Press

Russian

Novoe Vremia (New Time)
Rech (Spich)
Rossia (Russia)
St. Petersburg vedomosty (St. Petersburg News)
Odesskie Novosty (Odessa News)

Chinese

Beitsin zhibao (Peking)
Beitsin zhoubao (Peking Review)
Lishi yantsu (The Study of History)

English

Beijing Review
China Quarterly
Pioneer
Morning Star
The Times